LINGO

a course on words and how to use them

Lingo

BY ADRIAN SPOONER

Bristol Classical Press

First published in 1988 by
Bristol Classical Press
an imprint of
Gerald Duckworth & Co. Ltd.
The Old Piano Factory
48 Hoxton Square, London N1 6PB

Reprinted 1991

A CIP catalogue record for this book is available
from the British Library

ISBN 1-85399-031-0

Printed in Great Britain by
Billing and Sons Ltd, Worcester

Contents

Unit 1   The Greeks   page 1

Unit 2   Chaos   page 10

Unit 3   Kronos   page 21

Unit 4   Zeus   page 34

Unit 5   Hera   page 46

Unit 6   Demeter   page 57

Unit 7   Apollo   page 69

Unit 8   Artemis   page 79

Unit 9   Hermes   page 88

Unit 10   Hephaestus   page 99

Unit 11   Athene   page 110

Unit 12   Ares   page 122

Unit 13   Aphrodite   page 134

Unit 14   Poseidon   page 144

Unit 15   Dionysus   page 156

Acknowledgements

I am grateful to the University of Newcastle upon Tyne for granting me a Schoolmaster Fellowship, and to the Educational Department there for making accessible its facilities and expertise.

Special thanks must go to the Department of Classics, which was my home for a term. Head of Department John Lazenby, members of the department and students were unstintingly hospitable.

The help I received from Professor West, Dr. J.G.F. Powell and Dr. P.V. Jones is inestimable. Their advice and encouragement exceeded what I could have decently requested. Many thanks also to the illustrator, Christine Hall.

AJS

The publishers wish to acknowledge the following sources of photographs:
John H. Betts, p. 34
The Mansell Collection, pp. 2, 69, 88, 101, 126, 139
Sheila Maurice, pp. 2, 3
Mount Wilson and Las Campanas Observatories, Carnegie Institution of Washington, p. 14
The National Gallery, London, p. 159

Unit 1: The Greeks

1. THE GREEKS

Greece is a land of mountain ranges, plains and valleys. The people we call "Greeks" had not always lived there. Originally they came from western Asia, but found Greece a suitable place to settle. They were immigrants.

1. If you chose to settle in a land like Greece, where would you live? In the mountains or in the plains? Give some reasons for your answer.

1.

2. We know a lot about the ancient Greeks from vase paintings. What does this picture tell us about Greek farming?

2.

3. Greek farmers also grew olive trees. What do you think they used olives for?

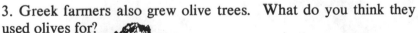

3.

4. The next picture, also taken from a Greek pot, tells you another skill the Greeks developed. What is it?

Look at your map of the Greek world. Can you see why this skill should be so important to the Greeks? Look carefully at the coastline of Greece. What advantages and dangers would a coastline like this offer?

4.

If you went to the "Greek section" of a museum, what things would you see there? Would you expect to see more of one sort of thing than any other? If you think so, what would it be, and why do you think that is the case?

5 & 6. These pictures come from Greek pots. What arts and crafts are depicted here?

5.

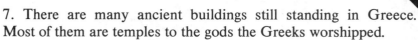

6.

7. There are many ancient buildings still standing in Greece. Most of them are temples to the gods the Greeks worshipped.

8. Much later, architects rediscovered the beauty of this style, and many buildings in our great cities look a bit like Greek temples.

7.

8.

9. At times the Greeks had to defend their own land. Sometimes they attacked other peoples'. What weapons are being used in the picture?

9.

10 & 11. What do you think is our most important source of knowledge about the Greeks?

The Greek reads ΒΟΡΟΣ ΕΙΜΙ ΤΗΣ ΑΟΡΑΣ HOROS EIMI TES AGORAS, and means "I am the boundary of the meeting place." The letters are slightly different from those you will see because the Greek alphabet changed its form.

The Greek below ΜΕΤ' ΙΗΣΟΥ, means "with Jesus". This is not a building but a memorial set up to one person. In what kind of place might you find this?

10.

11.

Exercise 1

Look at pictures 2 and 3.

The Latin word *agricultura* means "tending the fields".

Write down an English word you think we get from the Latin.

Now you will be given some Latin and Greek words connected with what you see in picture 4. See if you can complete the English column with words which come from them. The first one is done for you as an example.

<u>Latin</u>

mare, sea, *maritimus*, to do
  with the sea.

<u>English</u>

marine, (sub)marine,
maritime

Now you do these:

<u>Latin</u>

navis, ship, *navalis*, to do with
  a ship.

<u>Greek</u>

naus, ship, *nautikos*, to do
  with a ship.

Now try the same with the contents of pictures 5 and 6.

<u>Latin</u>

ars, skill, *artifex*, skilled
  person.
sculptura, carving.
sculptor, carver.
statua, image, monument.
pictura, a painting.

<u>Greek</u>

technē, skill, *technikos*,
  skilled.
graphē, picture, *graphikos*,
to do with painting.

And now with pictures 7 and 8:

Latin

architectura, the art of
  building.
architectus, a master builder.
templum, a holy building.
columna, a pillar.

Greek

architektōn, a master builder.

Refer to picture 9.

Latin

miles, soldier, *militaris*, of a
  soldier.
arma, weapons.
gladius, sword.

Greek

stratēgos, general. *stratēgikos*,
  like a general.
taktikos, ordering in a battle.

Finally, look at picture 10.

Latin

littera, a letter (of the alphabet).
verbum, a word.
scribo, I write. *scriptum*, a
  written thing.

Greek

gramma, a letter (of the
  alphabet).
logos, a word. *logikos,* to do
  with words.
graphō, I write, draw. *graphikos*,
  to do with writing, drawing.

The Gods

You may have heard of the Greek gods and some of their
adventures. The Greeks believed in many gods. They preferred
to believe that there was one god for each aspect of life, so that if
you needed help of a particular kind you knew who to ask. Here
are the gods and goddesses who looked after the parts of ancient
life we have been considering.

*Athene, goddess of arts and crafts,
and Poseidon, god of the sea*

*Demeter, goddess of things that grow
in the earth*

Ares, god of war

2. WORDPLAY: "What's the Time?"

When we say "This happened in 1500 c.e." we mean that it
happened 1500 years after the year 0. The letters "c.e." mean
"current era", that is, the present time rather than the past.

The letters "b.c.e." mean "before the current era". That is, all
the time before the year 0. So 1500 b.c.e. means 1500 years
before the year 0.

The line in the diagram below has the year 0 in the middle.
Everything on the left is time b.c.e. Everything on the right is
time c.e.

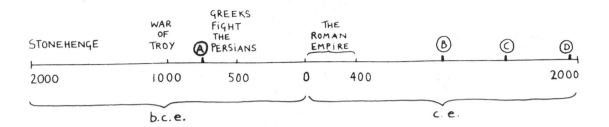

Exercise 1

Some great events of history have been marked on the line. Four other points have been marked on the line as A, B, C, D. Give the correct letter to each of the following events of history.
1) The Normans invade England, 1066 c.e.
2) You now.
3) The foundation of Rome, 753 b.c.e.
4) Christopher Columbus sights America, 1492 c.e.

Exercise 2

What year comes after 1987 c.e.?
What year comes after 500 b.c.e.?
What year comes before 1987 c.e.?
What year comes before 500 b.c.e.?

"Current" comes from the Latin word *currens* which means "running" or "going on now". It also applies to the flow of electricity or a river.

"Era" comes from the Latin word *aera*. This was a bronze counter that could be used in calculation.

3. GRAMMAR

"A, B, C . . ."

The Greek alphabet is beautiful and important. It gives us the word "alphabet" from its first two letters. It is part of the language of scientists and mathematicians.

Letter	Name	English
α	alpha	a
β	beta	b
γ	gamma	g
δ	delta	d
ε	epsilon	e (as in "get")
ζ	zeta	z (sd)
η	ēta	ē (as in "where")
θ	theta	th
ι	iota	i (as in "hit")
κ	kappa	k, c (as in "cat")
λ	lamda	l
μ	mu	m
ν	nu	n
ξ	xi	x
ο	omicron	o (as in "got")
π	pi	p
ρ	rho	r
σ, ς	sigma	s
τ	tau	t
υ	upsilon	u (also = y in English
φ	phi	ph
χ	chi	ch (as in Scottish "loch")
ψ	psi	ps
ω	omega	ō (as in "sword")

1) To get an H sound at the beginning of a word write ' over the first letter: ἑν ("hen") means "one". Rho at the beginning of a word always carries this mark: ῥ

2) Two gammas together are pronounced -ng: αγγελος ("angelos") = messenger, angel.

3) A line written above the letters e or o show that it makes the long sound, so that ē must be ēta, and the ō must be ōmega:

4) The form ς is only used at the end of a word, e.g. στρατηγος ("stratēgos") = general, man in charge of strategy.

e	=	ε	(epsilon)
ē	=	η	(eta)
o	=	ο	(omicron)
ō	=	ω	(omega)

Exercise 1: Using the Greek Alphabet

Many English words are simply Greek put into English letters. For example, the Greek for "drama" is δραμα, "basis" is βασις.

Write out the following words in Greek letters. Remember a line over ē or ō means it must be *ēta* or *ōmega*. English y is a Greek u.

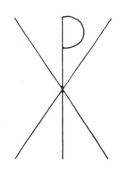

genesis   analysis
mētropolis   acropolis
iris   paralysis
nectar   horizōn
rhododendron   catastrophē

Look at the sign on the right. The Greek letters chi and rho, written thus, were used as a secret sign by early Christians. They stood for the first two letters of χριστος, the Greek for Christ.

Exercise 2: Latin Words

The Latin alphabet is the same as English (we got our letters from the Romans), so some Latin words will be the same in English:

medium (Latin) = medium
consul (Latin) = consul
minister (Latin) = minister
curriculum (Latin) = curriculum

Most Latin words, however, will have a different ending from the English:

libero = I liberate
curo = I cure
exspectatio = expectation
libertas = liberty

We get "bus" from the Latin omnibus, *which means "for everybody"*

What do you think the following Latin words mean?

honestas   *terminus*
imitatio   *velocitas*
fortuna   *causa*
materia   *monstrum*
neglectio   *elephantus*
palma   *signum*
sacrificium   *mentio*

Amanda is Latin for "lovable"

Unit 2: Chaos

1. CHAOS

What existed before the universe was created? Before there was any earth, sky, sea, planets, stars? If you say "nothing", it is difficult to imagine what all those things were made of. You try to imagine "nothing".

The Greeks believed there was something before the universe was created. They called it **Chaos.** The word means a great gaping yawn, a deep black hole. What the Greeks meant by Chaos here was all those things that were to make up the universe, but with no order. Everything was just swirling about in endless darkness, waiting for an accident to pull everything into order. The Greek for order is **Kosmos.**

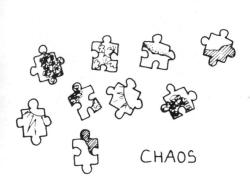

CHAOS

KOSMOS

This is how the Greek poet Hesiod tells the story of creation:

From Chaos Mother Earth was the first to appear, then Divine Love.

Next came Tartarus (Hell) buried deep within Mother Earth.

Then there was black Night, and Erebus, the dark way into Tartarus.

Night was female, Erebus male, and Divine Love brought the couple together.

Night gave birth to Day and Space, and then to Heaven. It was Earth and Heaven who together made all the natural features of the world.

Pontus was made next. He was all the sea which covers Mother Earth.

Father Heaven and Mother Earth then produced a family we know as the Titans, the youngest of whom was Kronos. Amongst the children there were the Cyclopes, the one-eyed giants, and other monsters, some with 100 hands and 50 heads.

Father Heaven hated those children of his who were monsters, and he thrust them back deep within Mother Earth. This caused her such pain, both mental and physical, that she persuaded Kronos to take action. She gave him a sickle with a blade of sharpened flint, and told him to lie in wait for Father Heaven.

As Night came, and Heaven spread himself over Earth, Kronos leapt on him and cut him with the sickle, slashing away again and again at his naked limbs. As the blood flowed it sprinkled Earth beneath, and a new race of giants was born from the drops. Aphrodite, the goddess of human passion, was also born then.

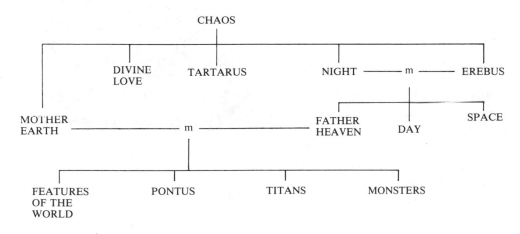

The people of India had different ideas about the creation of the universe. Here is one of their stories.

In the beginning the universe was a dark expanse containing nothing. The Lord of the universe decided it should be populated somehow, so he created the waters, and put a seed into them. This seed developed into an egg. The egg cracked, and the top of it became heaven, while the bottom part was the earth. There also appeared the Purusha, the first creature of the universe. It had a thousand faces, eyes, feet, arms, and contained everything that would go to make up the universe. The gods and demons sacrificed the creature. From its mouth came the class of priests and holy men, the gods and goats. The seasons were born from its armpits, merchants and cattle came from the thighs, while workers, horses and the earth itself came from its feet.

This comes from China:

Before heaven or earth were made, there was only chaos, which looked like an egg. P'an Ku was born in this egg. The heavy part of the egg became earth, while the light part of it was heaven. As heaven moved away from earth, so did P'an Ku grow. When he died, his eyes became the sun and moon, his flesh turned into the waters on the earth and his hair became the various plants.

P'an Ku

The Yoruba tribe of West Africa tell a story like this:

Obtala was Father Heaven, Odudua was Mother Earth. Father Heaven covered Mother Earth, who subsequently gave birth to children. One was Aganju, which means dry land. Wet land was represented by Yemaja. They had a son, Orungan, who fell in love with his mother. She bore sixteen children who became the great gods who were responsible for all human activity.

The Zuni Indians of New Mexico tell this story of creation:

In the first place there was only the creator, Awonawilona. As the creator of everything, he decided to turn himself into the sun. Father Sun rubbed his skin until lumps came off, and these became Mother Earth and Father Sky. Sky lay over Mother Earth, and she gave birth to all living things. Then they part, and Father Sky rules all heaven, Mother Earth all the things we see around us.

The Bible tells us that God created the universe in the following order:

	Day
Heaven, Earth, Waters Darkness (Night), Light (Day)	1
Sky (to separate Heaven and Earth)	2
Dry Land, Trees and Plants	3
Sun, Moon, Stars	4
Fish, Birds	5
Land Animals, People	6

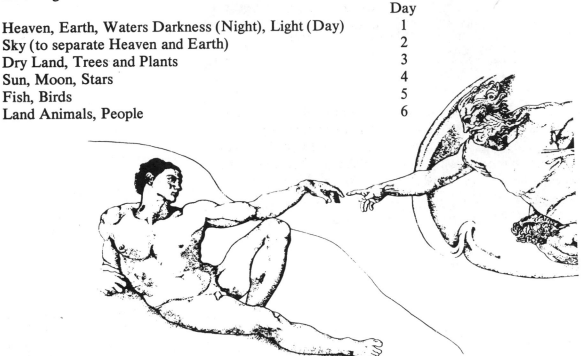

The science we call Cosmology (**kosmos,** order, **logos,** the study of) describes the creation of the universe in the following way. See if you can spot any similarities to the myths you have already read.

In the beginning there was neither time nor space. They are a part of the universe, and so they were created when the universe was created. The whole mass of the universe was concentrated into a point which had no size. 15,000,000,000 years ago this point exploded, and space was created and time started. The mass of the universe stayed the same, but, because it became less concentrated, those parts thrown out by the explosion had size. These parts are the galaxies, stars and planets we see in the sky. The explosion was accompanied by great heat, but as space grew and things moved in it, they cooled. Gases were formed which combined to produce things. You know how hydrogen and oxygen combine to produce water. Most important for us was the formation of a molecule called DNA which is the basis for the formation of life.

A big bang and the universe has begun

Exercise 1

1)   What did the Greeks think existed before the universe was created?
2)   What do the Hindus say was the beginning of everything?
3)   How long does the Bible say it took God to create the world?
4)   What similiarity is there between the Hindu and the Chinese myths of creation?
5)   What similarity is there between the African and Red Indian creation myths?
6)   What things does the scientific explanation share with myths of creation?

Exercise 2

1)   The laws of science show the ways in which the universe is "kept in order". For instance, the law of gravity means that things, when dropped, fall to the earth. You know that metals expand when they get hot. Chemical elements combine to produce compounds. Plants use sun to grow. Imagine one of these laws of science were reversed. Describe what the universe would be like then.
2)   Why do people invent myths?
3)   Why do scientists want to know about the universe?
4)   Invent a creation myth of your own. Start with some form of chaos, and end with some form of order. Your myth can be as weird as you want, so long as one step of creation follows reasonably from another.

2. WORDPLAY: "What do we get next?"

The Greeks were amongst the first scientists of the western world because they thought about and tried to explain the natural events happening around them.

Scientia is the Latin word for "knowledge". But as you know, getting knowledge does not only happen in science lessons. Every lesson is dedicated to giving you some of what the Romans called *scientia*. Without knowing it, you actually use the English form of many Latin and Greek words every day.

One subject title on the timetable comes from Arabic. That is "Chemistry", from the Arabic *al kimia*, which means "changing the state of . . .". But the Arabs got that word from the Greeks. The Greek *chymeia* means "mixing metals".

Exercise 1

Take out your school timetable. Many of the subjects below will appear on it. The columns below give you the subject name, the Latin or Greek word that subject name comes from, and the meaning of the Latin or Greek word. E.g.:

Subject name	Latin	Greek	Meaning of ancient word
art	*ars*		skill
drama		*drama*	doing
music		*mousa*	a goddess who inspires the arts
technology		*technē*	skill
studies	*studium*		study, pursuit

Your job now is to fill in column 1 using the information you are given in the other columns. Your timetable will help you.

Subject name	Latin	Greek	Meaning of ancient word	
		physis	nature	(One subject title from *physis*,
	educare		to train	another from *physis* & *educare*)
	religio		religion	(combine with *studium*)
		bios	life	
		mathēma	a thing which is learned	
		gē	the earth	(two subjects)
		historia	enquiry	
		oikos	household	
	computo		I reckon	
	commercium		trade	

What about "English" and "French"?. The **Angli** originally lived in Germany. When they came to England they brought their language with them which helped shape the **English** we know. There is a Latin word *Franciscus* which means someone **from France.**

Ends of words

You will see from the exercise you have done that subject names start with a Greek or Latin word, onto which an ending is put.

gē = earth, add *(o)graphy* for *geography*.
bios = life, add *logy* for *biology*.

graphy and *logy* are called **suffixes**, meaning simply that they stuck on to the end of a word. Here are some others:

mathematICS
technicAL
geoLOGY
commerciAL

Unit 2: Chaos
Exercise 2

Here are some more studies which you probably don't do at school yet, although you may have heard of them.

This time, you will be given the English word, its English definition, and then the Latin or Greek word it derives from. See if you can think what the original Latin or Greek word means. E.g.:

English	Definition	Latin	Greek	Your guess
literature	something written	*littera*		a letter of the alphabet
theology	study of god		*theos*	god

Now you try to complete the last column:

English	Definition	Latin	Greek	Your guess
zoology	study of animals		*zōon*	
politics	how states work		*polis*	
sociology	how people behave in groups	*socius*		
botany	study of plants		*botanē*	
horticulture	use of a garden to produce flowers, vegetables etc.	*hortus*		
astronomy	study of the stars		*astron*	

Look back at the English words of the timetable and see if you can find a suffix which crops up several times.

The commonest is **-logy**, which comes from the Greek *logos* = "word". When used like this in English it means "study of", so "geology" means a study of the earth. Geologists are concerned with the rocks that make up the earth.

You may have noticed the suffix **-graphy**, from the Greek *graphō* = "I draw, write". So "geography" is drawing or writing about the earth.

The suffix **-nomy** is from the Greek *nomos* = "order, law". Thus astronomy is ordering or classifying the stars.

Exercise 3: Inventaword

Using your ancient words list and any suffixes you know, make up some subjects for study. They can be as silly as you like, but do use only ancient words to make them up. For instance, "Fishology" won't work, but if you use the Latin *piscis* (fish) and get "piscology", that would be fine. Define your studies once you have invented them. Here are some of mine:

populomontography	writing about people on mountains (you can use as many words as you want)
antiquology	a study of ancient things
zooclaustronomy	study of how to lock up animals

Using the Greek alphabet

Write the following words in Greek letters, and give their meaning in English. Remember that a letter with a line above it must be the long form of that letter (eta and omega):

physis, bios, mathēma, gē, historia, oikos, astron, theos, zōon, polis, botanē

3. GRAMMAR

People, Places and Things

Here is an item from a newspaper T.V. column advertising a programme. I have left some words out. See if you can add words to make the item sensible.

7.00 Wish You Were Here? _____ reports from _____, _____ goes on a Swiss cross-country skiing _____, Chris Kelly arrives in _____ on the second leg of a two-centre _____.

The missing words which appeared in the paper are given at the bottom of the page. It doesn't matter if your words were different, so long as the piece ends up making some sense.

Exercise 1: Anneka Rice. Blackpool. Judith Chalmers. Holiday. Bermuda. Holiday.

Try the same again with this piece:

There was a young _____ from Wapping,
Who helped his dear _____ with the _____.
While out in the _____
He heard a soul beat,
And dropping the _____ went bopping.

(Try to keep it clean!)

Different kinds of words in the English language have different jobs. We certainly need words which name things. Those are the kind of words you will have used to complete the passages above. We call these words **nouns** (from the Latin *nomen* = name). There are several kinds of noun:

1) **Proper noun** names a particular person, place or thing. It will often have a capital letter in English. Such nouns are Robert, London, Sarah, Mercedes Benz, Sony Walkman.

Exercise 1

Pick out the proper nouns from the following sentence:
Dracula stalked the streets of Neasden looking for a victim. Finding him was a job only Basil could do.

2) **Common noun**. Any person, place or thing, and not one in particular: person, town, car, tape recorder.

Exercise 2

Pick out the common nouns in the sentence given above.

3) **Collective nouns** name a group or class of things: flock (of sheep), litter (of puppies), band (of musicians).

Exercise 3

Find the collectives:
The herd of elephants, chasing Dracula down the street, drove him towards a couple of policemen who had just dealt with the gang of youths. Dracula lost his shoe in the chase.

4) **Abstract**: something that is not solid or material: happiness, fun, science, laughter.

Exercise 4

Look at the Chaos stories. Pick out
    10 common nouns
     8 abstract nouns
     5 proper nouns
     2 collective nouns

Exercise 5

Pick out one of each kind of noun from the following:
    There was a young fellow called Tony
    Whose knees were excessively boney.
    They caused so much humour
    That round went a rumour
    He'd borrowed a pair from a pony.

Unit 3: Kronos

1. KRONOS

Chaos had given way to Kosmos, and Kronos was its master. But
he had gained power by violence. Being violent had got him what
he wanted, and now he wanted Rhea. So he raped her, and in
nine months' time she gave birth to the first of her children. This
5   was Hestia, goddess of the hearth, who orders and protects the
home.

    Kronos knew only too well that what you get by violence can
be taken from you in the same way. He had even heard from
Heaven and Earth that his own children would rebel against him.
10 Knowing this there was nothing too monstrous, nothing too
horrific he would not do to keep his power.

    So Hestia had been born. Rhea, exhausted from the birth, but
full of pride because of the beauty and perfection of the baby,
nursed her in her arms. Kronos approached and asked to see the
15 child. He leaned over Hestia and smiled, and she smiled back at
her father. He touched her little hands, and the baby instinctively
grasped his finger and held tight.

    He turned to Rhea. "Can I pick her up and hold her a while?"
She had not forgotten the way he had given her the baby. The
20 horrible memory flashed through her mind, but she dismissed it.
She reckoned Kronos' hard heart had been softened. After all, he
was smiling and acting like a proud father. A baby this perfect,
this loveable, might calm his brutal soul.

    Rhea offered the baby to its father, and he carefully took it.
25 But men can be awkward things, and she did not let go until she
was sure that Kronos had her safe. "Be quiet and kind" she said.
Her voice was tremulous, but she was confident that the sight of
the child would tame Kronos. She smiled inwardly that a baby
could conquer a Titan.

30   A similar thought went through Kronos' mind. He
remembered something he had once been told; a chill ran through
his bones, but he did not show any fear in his face. He glowed
with paternal pride and kissed the child's head. He held it at
arms' length and muttered nonsense baby words as adults do. He
35 was pleased with what he and Rhea had created, but he could not
think of creating without also thinking of destruction. He still

smiled, but the smile seemed to have a different meaning behind
it. His face broke into a hideous grin as he drew the child closer
and closer. What happened then was incredible. Rhea saw it, but
40 did not believe her own eyes.

"This is not real," she told herself. "it is a nightmare." Even
when she heard the screams and saw the blood, she still did not
believe.

Kronos was swallowing the last of Hestia as he wiped the
45 blood from his beard. He showed no fatherly feelings now. He
just looked satisfied.

A threat had been removed, he thought. A good job had been
done. He gave Rhea one quick look, turned, and walked away.

Rhea's mind was in turmoil. She was hysterical; she was grief
50 stricken; she was bitter and wanted revenge. But Kronos did not
leave her to these feelings. Hestia was the first of many children
they had, and at each birth he made a new meal. Rhea grew more
and more frantic. Now pregnant for the sixth time, she was
determined that the child should survive. But where could she
55 turn? To her husband? No. Only her parents, Father Heaven
and Mother Earth could help.

Earth was a kind mother, and Heaven had no love for the son
who had given him such a vicious wound. And they saw
everything which happened in the universe. They would bring
60 help to Rhea, and Kronos to justice.

Rhea's sixth child was born. It was a fine new baby boy, but unlike any other child she had seen. He seemed to shine with wisdom and power, and she was determined that he would survive.

Hestia

65 Heaven and Earth took the baby from Rhea's arms. She did not want him to go, but she knew that if he stayed with her he would die. The child was taken to the island of Crete, and hidden in a cave deep within the mountains. This was the beginning of a plan which would defeat Kronos. He had to think that everything was as it had always been. He must not know that the child had been taken away. If he found out, the child would be in danger. Earth therefore gave Rhea a bundle to nurse. It looked just like a baby, but was, in fact, a stone wrapped up in infant clothes.

Rhea played her part well. She held the lifeless thing to her breast and sang to it. She showed terror as Kronos approached, clung to the bundle and did all she could to stop him taking it. She willingly suffered his violent attack on her, pleaded for the life of the child as Kronos, distracted by the weeping and wailing, swallowed the stone. It never crossed his mind that he had been fooled. He was used to getting his way by force. No strength had ever been greater than his; but for the first time he was confronted not with physical strength, but with cleverness.

Hera

Kronos thought he was safe again. Everything had happened to a pattern he knew well. But he was wrong.

85 Time went by and Rhea's baby, called Zeus, grew in strength and wisdom. The trap, devised long ago by Heaven and Earth, was now ready to be sprung.

Earth introduced Zeus to Kronos. He had no idea who the boy was, but was charmed by his wit and good looks. They talked a while, and Zeus, pretending to be hospitable, offered Kronos a drink. Kronos took the cup and swallowed the contents. The sweet taste of the wine covered the bitterness of the poison. He thought that this was the finest wine he had ever tasted, and asked for more. The wine at first put him in a jolly mood, but then he began to feel feverish. He was sweating, and could not focus his eyes on anything. The room began to spin, and a sharp pain in his stomach made him cry out. He gulped down air to stop himself being sick, but it was no use. The pain became unbearable, and he vomited all the contents of his stomach.

100 First came the stone, and then a stream of chewed up meat. Heaven and Earth breathed into these remains, and they showed signs of life. The pieces of meat began to tremble, and then

Hades

moved together. It was as though each piece knew where it belonged. Five recognisable shapes formed, now appearing like
105 young children. Then, gaining strength and size, they stood side by side with Zeus. Here were Kronos's children whom he had eaten. But now they were a monstrous army, sworn to revenge. They were powerful, but so was Kronos. But they were also wise, and Kronos had never faced such an enemy.

110 Zeus and his brothers and sisters withdrew. They freed the giants and monsters Kronos had thrown into chains, and the Cyclopes forged a destructive new weapon for Zeus: the thunderbolt. Kronos, now intent on war, called the Titans to his side.

115 The clash that followed unleashed all the power of the universe. Force was met with force and the battle was fierce. But force alone could not win the day. The Titans, not having the wisdom and cunning of their enemy, gave ground and fell. Their power, huge and uncontrolled, finally went for nothing against
120 strength guided by wisdom, and they lost the fight. Zeus and his brothers and sisters were the new gods, and a new age was born.

Demeter

Poseidon

Zeus

Exercise 1

1) How did Kronos discover that he might be attacked by his own children?
2) How did he try to prevent any such attack?
3) What was Rhea's trick to save Zeus?
4) What was the first Zeus saw of his brothers and sisters?
5) Who were the allies of a) Kronos and b) Zeus in the battle which followed?
6) Describe a battle between a Titan and a god. You may draw a picture.

The victory of Zeus and his allies brought new light to the universe, while the Titans were condemned to imprisonment under the earth. But there was still the danger of discord. The ancient gods had been prepared to kill for power, so why not the new ones? Zeus, god of brightness, sought a balance in the universe based on justice and agreement. He proposed a lottery to decide which god should rule over which part of the world. All the gods agreed on two things: they should all have a share of power on the earth, and they would stand by the result of the draw. As it turned out, Zeus received power over the heavens and became king of the gods. Poseidon the Earthshaker took the kingdom of the seas, while Hades had to be content to reign over the dead deep down in hell.

You may already know some stories about these gods. You may also be aware that the Romans gave them different names (after all they spoke a different language). Here is a list of the Roman gods:

Greek	Roman
Hestia	Vesta
Hera	Juno
Demeter	Ceres
Hades (also Pluto)	Orcus (also Dis)
Poseidon	Neptune
Zeus	Jupiter

You will notice that the god of the Underworld has several names. He was a god people tried to avoid mentioning because of his connection with death, and so they sought other ways of speaking about him.

Exercise 2

1) Write down anything you already know about any of the six children of Rhea. It doesn't matter whether you know them by their Greek or Roman name.

2) Why was Kronos so violent towards his children? Why were his children so violent towards him? Which of the two had more right on their side? Give some reasons for your answer.

3) Anything to do with the gods we call *divine*. Can you see, from this story, any differences between the way the Greeks thought about divine things and the way we do?

2. WORDPLAY

You know that before the universe was created there was no order to things at all. There are several ways in which you could describe this state: unorganised, disordered, messy, mixed up and so on.

The Greeks called this state of affairs *chaos*, and they could best describe this state by calling it *chaotikos*.

Try to find an English word which comes from this Greek word which you could use to describe your bedroom when it needs tidying, or perhaps even the school corridor at the end of the day. The English word you get is *chaotic*.

Chaos is a **noun** because it names something. But *chaotic* describes something, and because a describing word does a different job from a noun, it must be called something different.

The Latin word *adjectus* means "added". The **adjective** *adds* meaning to the noun. So *chaotic bedroom* tells you more than *bedroom*.

DRIVE WITH CARE

ROAD AHEAD

CHAOTIC!

Exercise 1

How many adjectives can you find in the following sentence — i.e. words to describe something or someone, rather than name it. Answers at the bottom of the page.

    Superman is a super man who wears a blue suit, red pants and a red cape, and helps poor and defenceless people against others who are powerful and bad.

Exercise 2: (Blue) Peter

Some adjectives are so regularly associated with a noun that they can hardly be separated from it. Consider:

    "The *yellow* rose of Texas."

Remove the adjective and you no longer have a "well known phrase".

super, blue, red, poor, defenceless, powerful, bad

What adjective do you need to turn the following into a well known phrase, title etc?

The _____ Pimpernel.
The _____ Max.
The _____ Baron.
James Bond, _____ agent.
The _____ Ranger.
A _____ step for mankind.
The _____ Show on Earth.

Exercise 3: Adjectives that Help

Adjectives also give us more information which may be necessary for a proper understanding of a sentence:
   . . . and the sky is not *cloudy* all day.

What adjective is missing from the following? If you have not met the sentence before, think of a good adjective to fill the gap:
   We all live in a _____ submarine.
   The Minstrel Boy to the War is gone.
      With his _____ harp slung behind him.
   God save our _____ Queen.
   There is a _____ hill far away.

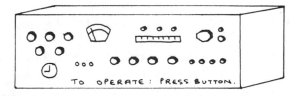

Exercise 4: Adjectives you Need

Adjectives can also give information necessary to do something. A department store might refer to certain goods being on the Ground Floor, First Floor etc. What would you do without the adjective?

   Instructions to operate a control panel would be useless without adjectives. Imagine your computer manual said:
   "To start programme press button. To stop programme, press button. Search programme, press button. To brighten display, press button."

Here is a recipe. What must you add to get any useful sense from it?
   "Take _____ ounces of flour, and add a _____ pinch of salt.
   Stir until well mixed. Add _____ eggs and _____ pint of milk.

Beat until you get a _____ mixture. Leave to stand for three hours, until the mixture becomes _____, and then cook for 30 minutes at a _____ temperature."

Try to think of other kinds of instructions it would be impossible to follow if adjectives were removed from those instructions.

Exercise 5: Vital Adjectives

Finally, adjectives can give you vital information which is, literally, a matter of life and death.

Look at the first road sign. The instruction not to turn right is clear. It is crucial to know that the forbidden turn is *right*.

Complete the warnings on the rest of the signs.

ROAD   CHIPPINGS.

STOP WHEN
____ LIGHT
SHOWS

DANGER
_____
VOLTAGE

____ BRIDGE
____ HEADROOM
14 FEET

CAUTION
VEHICLE

Exercise 6: Naming Adjectives

Adjectives in English which end in -ic or -tic, like *chaotic*, have copied the Greek adjective ending *-ikos*. The same is true of adjectives which end in -ical or -tical, like *magical*, *statistical*.

Using a dictionary if necessary, write down the meaning of the following words:
    comical
    medical
    logical
    optimistic
    pessimistic
    static
    physical
    astronomical
    economical

" THE WEATHER WILL CLEAR IN A MINUTE OR TWO."

When you have done that, look at the following ancient words. Match each one to its adjective (G = Greek, L = Latin):
    oikos (G)   house
    pessimus (L)   worst
    physis (G)   nature
    stare (L)   to stand
    medicus (L)   doctor

logos (G)   word
astron (G)   star
optimus (L)   best
komoidia (G)   comedy

Exercise 7

You will find below three columns of words, English, Greek, and Latin. Turn the nouns into an English adjective ending in -tic, -ic, -tical, -ical. E.g., Greek: *topos*, a place. English adjective: *topical*.

English	Greek	Latin
idiot	*drama* (doing)	*magus* (wise man)
alcohol	*arithmos* (number)	*majestas* (greatness)
terrify	*methodos* (way)	*luna* (moon)
nonsense	*chronos* (time)	*civis* (citizen)
practice	*typos* (pattern)	*poeta* (poet)
pirate	*anaisthesia* (lack of feeling)	*aqua* (water)

Exercise 8: Making More Adjectives

There are other suffixes which make a word into an adjective. The following all come to us from the Latin language and give a particular sense to the adjective:

-ible and -able, "able to be". Manage*able* means "able to be managed".

-ant and -ent, describes a state or condition: abs*ent*: "not being here".

-ous and -ive, having some characteristic: mass*ive*: "having mass".

E.g. the radio is *portable*, the food *edible*, the teacher *monstrous*, Christmas *festive*, I am *extravagant*, and the mark is *permanent*.

Using the word endings given above, turn the following into adjectives. If you get confused, use a dictionary.

eat, horror, vigour, differ, extend, irritate.

Exercise 9

Go through the story of Kronos, and find an example of each type of adjective we have been looking at. Write down the adjective with its line number, underline the suffix only, and then say what the adjective means.

Exercise 10

The work you have done should now help you to say what the following Latin adjectives mean. E.g. *horribilis* means "horrible", *constans* means "constant". Now try these:

    captivus
    neglegens
    infans
    incredibilis
    sociabilis
    jocosus
    prominens
    propheticus
    proportionalis
    provocativus
    rationalis

VERY JOCOSUS, BUT YOU ARE STILL CAPTIVUS!

3. GRAMMAR

Exercise 1: Using the Greek Alphabet

The adjective ending -ic, -ical comes from the Greek adjective ending *-ikos*. For instance, the Greek word παθητικος means pathetic.

Write the following Greek adjectives in Greek letters. The meaning of the word is given in brackets:

    politikos   (political)
    oikonomikos   (economic)
    idiōtikos   (private)
    dramatikos   (dramatic)
    historikos   (historical)

Exercise 2

Now read these Greek words, and see if you can write down what they mean:

μαθηματιχος
ενεργγητιχος
φανταστιχος
δραστιχος
χρονιχος
χοσμητιχος
στρατηγιχος

Exercise 3

You know that a noun is a word which names someone or something. Adjectives are words which describe a noun. For example, *school* is a noun, but there are any number of adjectives you could use to describe it: lovely, horrible, exciting, boring, funny, dull.

How would you describe school? Think of five adjectives *you* think do the job.

The power of adjectives

Adjectives can make a vital difference to the meaning of a sentence. For example:

"The man received a parcel": this simply tells you a fact with no hint of how or why. Then try adding some adjectives:

"The trembling man received the unexpected parcel": this suggests that something nasty is going to happen. What could be in the parcel, and why is the man frightened?

"The happy man received the exciting parcel": this sentence has a different feeling altogether.

Exercise 4

Here is a passage from Hesiod's description of the battle between the Gods, helped by the Giants, and the Titans. Hesiod wrote about two thousand five hundred years ago. In a long poem he tells of the birth of the universe, the Titans and the Gods and about their incredible powers.

The adjectives have been left out of this version. You rewrite the passage using adjectives wherever you think they will improve the telling of the story.

"A hundred arms sprang from the Giants' shoulders, and they had fifty heads. The Giants drew themselves up against the Titans in battle, wielding boulders.

On the other side the Titans strengthened their battle line, and both sides showed what they could do by force.

The sea gave a roar and the earth re-echoed. Olympus shook from its foundations as the Gods charged, and the quaking reached into hell."

Exercise 5: Weird

And finally . . .

Here is a poem by Lewis Carroll called *Jabberwocky*. It is called a nonsense poem, and you will quickly see why.

Read it through, and pick out five words you think might be adjectives. Then say what you think they might mean.

Jabberwocky

'Twas brillig and the slithy toves
Did gyre and gimble in the wabe;
All mimsy were the borogoves,
And the mome raths outgrabe.

"Beware the Jabberwock, my son!
The jaws that bite, the claws that catch!
Beware the Jubjub bird, and shun
the frumious Bandersnatch!"

He took his vorpal sword in hand;
Long time the manxome foe he sought—
So rested he by the Tumtum tree
And stood awhile in thought.

And as in uffish thought he stood,
The Jabberwock, with eyes of flame,
Came whiffling through the tulgey wood,
And burbled as it came!

One, two! One, two! And through and through
The vorpal blade went snicker-snack!
He left it dead, and with its head
He went galumpging back.

And hast though slain the Jabberwock!
Come to my arms my beamish boy!
O frabjous day! Callooh! Callay!"
He chortled in his joy.

'Twas brillig and the slithy toves
Did gyre and gimble in the wabe;
All mimsy were the borogoves,
And the mome raths outgrabe.

Unit 4: Zeus

1. ZEUS

A single blow of the axe brought the ox to the ground. Prometheus then picked up a sharp, curved knife and showed the people how to carve the carcase to separate the good, eatable meat from the innards and bones.

5   Prometheus was a Titan who had proved himself a good friend to man.   A quick thinker (his name means "one who thinks ahead"), he was the ideal teacher of mortals who, in these early days, had few skills to boast of.

The final stage of this lesson would be how to cook the meat
10 of the animal. Prometheus knew that Zeus, king of gods and men,
ruler of heaven and wielder of the thunderbolt, would demand his
share of the carcase once it was fully prepared, and he feared that
men would be left with the less appetising parts after Zeus had
made his choice.

15 So he stripped the hide off the animal, and made it into two
bags. Into one he placed all the good, lean meat, but was careful
to put the stomach on top to hide it. In the other bag he placed
the bones and the offal and all those parts you would not want to
eat. Prometheus then invited Zeus to attend their gathering.

20 "Here before you, Zeus, are two bags containing all the parts
of the butchered ox. You choose whichever of the bags you want,
and the people will be content with whatever is left over in the
other one."

Zeus considered the offer. One bag was certainly much bigger
25 than the other. It must contain more meat; and he was, after all,
king of gods and men, and it was only right that he should have
the greater share. So Zeus took the bigger bag and made off for
Olympus.

When he opened the bag, however, he got a shock. He found
30 bones, hooves, horns, eyes, guts, everything he would not consider
eating. And on top of this discovery a delicious smell started his
mouth watering and stomach rumbling in the expectation of a fine
feast. He looked down to earth and saw that the mortals had all
the good meat spitted and roasting gently over charcoal fires. It
35 was bad enough that mortals should be tucking into good
succulent steaks without him. What could not be forgiven was
that he had been tricked. Nor was he tricked in private. It wasn't
as though nobody knew what had happened. Everybody knew
that they were enjoying their feast because Zeus had been palmed
40 off with a bag of inferior meat. These mere mortals had to be
taught a painful lesson, and quickly, or Zeus stood to lose their
respect.

Back on earth the people had fallen into the party spirit. They
talked and laughed, eating or watching the meat turn on the spits,
45 sizzling as it cooked and giving off the most wonderful aroma.

Then something strange started to happen. The fire over
which the meat was cooking began to fail. However much fuel
they put on it, however hard they blew the flame to keep it going,
it continued to die. Finally the charcoal merely glowed, and that
50 glow became less and less intense. Soon it was cold - as cold as

the uncooked meat stuck uselessly on the spits.

The people made for their homes, confused by what had happened. Why had the fire in the hearth gone out? And why was it impossible to light it again? No method they knew would
55 produce a flame.

Without fire the nights became dark and cold. Food had to be eaten raw, and wild animals again began to gather around their homes. In short, life returned to the hard job of day to day survival they had known in the past.
60 But Prometheus knew full well what had happened. Zeus had taken the fire to remind people of his superiority, and to punish them for their part in tricking him.

So Prometheus went up to Olympus and stole a ray from the sun. He hid this in the hollow stalk of a plant and slipped back to
65 earth unseen. The fire had returned!

The king of the gods misses nothing, and he was soon aware that people had heat and light again. Now he had been tricked twice. Prometheus would be punished in such a way that mortals and gods alike would never forget that he was their master.
70 Prometheus' punishment must be a lesson to all.

Zeus instructs the eagle

Prometheus was taken by force to a mountain far away in the Caucasus. Heavy chains were fixed deep into the side of the mountain, and Prometheus was shackled there hand and foot. As he hung there, he became aware of an eagle circling above him.
75 Lower and lower it flew, getting ever closer to Prometheus. Now it hung in the air opposite him, and cast a huge shadow over his body. Then it settled, digging its hooked claws into his side to get a good hold. Searing pain shot through Prometheus' body as the eagle ripped the flesh of his side with its sharp, hooked beak. It
80 buried its head deep within his body until it located his liver. It ate the liver. It took all day and Prometheus never lost consciousness.

At the end of the day, the great bird departed, leaving Prometheus hanging mutilated on the rock face. But during the
85 night a miracle happened. The liver began to grow again inside his body. By the morning it was whole again.

Then Prometheus looked up and saw a sight which struck terror into him. It was not long before the eagle had settled again, enjoying the same meal it had eaten the day before.
90 This is how the solitary years passed for Prometheus. He had deceived Zeus and was condemned to what seemed eternal torture.

Mortals too were punished. Prometheus had protected the human race by locking up all its evils in a jar. He had bottled up
95 Old Age, Hard Work, Illness, Madness, Sin, Anger, Envy and Viciousness and all those diseases and emotions which make life bad. Zeus sent the woman Pandora amongst people. She opened the jar and released all those things which could hurt the human race. Ever since then we have suffered hurt, unhappiness and
100 war. But one thing remained in the jar available to people in the face of all these horrors. It was something which might make all the evils we have to face tolerable. It is called Hope.

There was hope for Prometheus too. Herakles, a son of Zeus, saw Prometheus on his travels. He knew why he was there, but
105 took pity on him. Praying that Zeus would understand and forgive his act of kindness, Herakles shot the eagle dead and freed Prometheus from his torment.

Exercise 1

1) What weapon could Zeus use against his enemies?
2) How was Zeus tricked first?
3) How did he punish people for this trickery?
4) Who helped mortals out of this terrible situation?
5) How was he punished for giving this help?
6) How did he finally escape this punishment?

Exercise 2

1) Why should Zeus be an appropriate god for the Greeks?
2) Are there any examples in this story of gods behaving in the same way as mortals? How would the story change if they reacted differently?
3) Who was the better friend to mortals? Zeus or Prometheus? Did Zeus act simply to hurt people? If not, what reasons could he have had?
4) You may have heard about Frankenstein's monster. The book *Frankenstein* was written by Mary Shelley. She gave it a subtitle: *A Modern Prometheus*. Why do you think she decided on this title?
5) Imagine you could remove from the earth those things which hurt and trouble people most. What would be your first five items to be removed? Why have you picked these?

2. WORDPLAY

Different Languages . . .

Even if you haven't heard of Zeus before doing this course, you may have heard of Jupiter. This is what the Romans called Zeus. Why should the same person have a different name?

The obvious reason is that Greek and Latin are different languages. We call England "England"; the French call it "Angleterre". We call Germany "Germany"; the French call it "Allemagne"; the Germans call it "Deutschland".

Which would you say was the proper name of the country we call Germany? Or are they all equally good?

Sometimes different languages have names for the same thing that look similar to each other. We have the word *cat* as the name of this animal:

    A Frenchman would call it *chat*.
    An Italian would say *gatto*.
    A Spaniard would say *gato*.
    A German would say *Katze*.
    A Welsh speaker would say *cath*.

. . . From One Source

Why arc all these words similar? The answer is that they all have the same origin. They all come from a Latin word for cat, *cattus*.

Can we find a link between the names Zeus and Jupiter?

People who study languages think that most European languages come from a very ancient tongue we call Indo-European (because some Indian languages come from it too). This was originally spoken in Central Asia. When people moved from there to parts of Europe and Asia, they continued to speak that language. But as you have seen with "cat", different nationalities change their language, and say what was originally the same word in a different way.

The ancient Indian, using the language called Sanskrit, would call God "Father of light". or *Dyauh pitar*. A Greek would say *Zeu pater*, and a Roman *Jupiter*.

If you try saying these words to yourself you might see how similar you can make *Zeu pater* and *Jupiter* sound. Notice too how the Greeks dropped the "fathcr" part of the word (*pater*) and came to refer to God as Zeus.

Exercise 1

Can you find any English words which might come from *pitar*, *pater*, *piter*? Use your dictionary carefully, and check that the word you find has something to do with fathers. The *pater* form is the one to concentrate on.

Exercise 2: Gods . . .

Look at this list of Roman names for Greek gods:

Greek	Latin
Hermes	Mercurius (or Mercury)
Aphrodite	Venus
Ares	Mars
Zeus	Jupiter
Kronos	Saturnus (or Saturn)
Poseidon	Neptunus (or Neptune)

English uses the names of the Roman gods to refer to something quite different. Where might you find these names being used?

You might know some names missing from this list. Uranus and Pluto are Greek names spelled the Latin way. These two planets, and Neptune too, were not known to the ancients, but were given classical names when they were discovered.

Exercise 3 . . . in Heaven

You now find yourself in the world of the "astronomer" (someone who studies the stars and other heavenly bodies).

  The Greek word *astron* means "star", and *nomos* means "ordering" or "classifying". According to other stories the Greeks tell, we find that Prometheus was a mathematician and astronomer.

The Greek word *planēs* (pronounced *plan-airs*) means a "wanderer". What English word comes from that? Is it a good word to use for that purpose? Think what planets do in space.

Exercise 4

As in most sciences, astronomy takes its technical terms from
Latin and Greek.

Here are some Latin and Greek words with their meaning.
What English word, to do with astronomy, comes from each one?

Latin   Greek

luna   (moon)   *astron*   (star)
satelles   (attendant)   *gala*   (milk)
sol   (sun)
orbis   (circle)
stella   (star)

When you have found the English word, try to connect it with the
meaning of the ancient word. E.g. *luna*: we get "lunatic". People
believed that a full moon could turn people mad. Remember,
some people turn into werewolves on the night of the full moon.

A constellation is a group of stars. The **prefix** *con* means
"together", and you know *stella*. We give constellations names in
accordance with the shape they seem to make in the sky.

Exercise 5

Here are four constellations as they are seen in the night sky.
Each one has a Latin name. Look for a shape made by the star
groups. You might want to experiment by joining up the dots in
certain ways. What you should do is match up the constellation
with the Latin name. The names are: *Canis Major* (Bigger Dog),
Gemini (Twins), *Leo* (Lion), *Scorpio* (Scorpion).

Exercise 6: Words in Maths

Prometheus was a mathematician, and the Greeks were amongst the first to make a proper study of the subject. That is why many words used in maths come from Greek. There are also many which come from Latin. The Greek word *mathema* means "something learned".

But let's start with "Arithmetic". The Greek word *arithmos* means "number". What branch of maths does arithmetic deal with?

Below you will find some Latin words with their meanings. What English words used in arithmetic do we get from them?

addo	I place one thing with another
subtraho	I take one thing from another (*subtractus* means "taken away")
multiplico	I increase something
divido	I share, distribute
frango	I break something up (*fractus* means "broken")
decimus	A tenth part of something
per centum	Out of a hundred
calculus	A stone used in reckoning (like those a cricket umpire uses)
productus	Lengthened
quotiens	How many times?

Exercise 7

Now let us look at the words used in measurement.

The Greek word *metron* means a "measure" or a "rule". Hence the word we use for the basic unit of length, the "metre".

Here are the Greek and Latin words for round numbers to 1000.

	Latin	Greek
10	*decem* (deci-)	*deka*
100	*centum* (centi-)	*hekaton* (hecto-)
1000	*mille* (milli-)	*chilioi* (kilo-)

In the metric system we use the Latin **prefix** for fractions of a metre, the Greek prefix for multiples of a metre.

For instance: 1/10 of a metre is a "<u>deci</u>metre", using the Latin prefix. 10 times a metre is a "<u>deka</u>metre", using the Greek prefix. What is the proper word for:

1/100 of a metre?	100 times a metre?
1/1000 of a metre?	1000 times a metre?

1.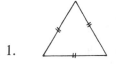

Exercise 8: Geometry

2.

You know the Greek word *gē*, and also *metron*. So define "geometry". This term is applied in maths to measuring the sides and angles of figures. A figure commonly dealt with is the triangle. The Latin *tres anguli* means "three angles", which, of course, every triangle has. The study of triangles is called "trigonometry". *Tri* is from the Greek for 3. *Gōnia* is the Greek for "angles". *Metron* you already know. *Poly-* comes from the Greek meaning "many". So define a *polygon*.

3.

How many angles do the following figures have? Pentagon, hexagon, heptagon, octagon, nonagon, decagon.

4.

The Latin words *aequa latera* mean "equal sides". Describe an equilateral triangle (1).

Isos is the Greek for "equal". *Skelos* is the Greek for "leg". Describe an isosceles triangle (2).

5.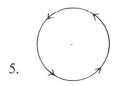

The dotted line chops triangle 3 in half. The Latin *bis* means "twice". *Sectus* means "cut". What is the mathematical term for cutting a figure in two?

Finally, let us look at mathematical words used about "circles" (Latin: *circulus*).

Here are some Latin and Greek terms. Match the description a, b, c, d, with one of the drawings on the right.

6.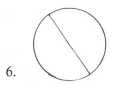

a) *Radius* (Latin, "a spoke"): radius
b) *Dia* (Greek, "across") *metron* ("measure"): diameter
c) *Circum* (Latin, "around") *ferens* (Latin, "carrying"): circumference
d) *Tangens* (Latin, "touching"): tangent

7.

3. GRAMMAR

Exercise 1

Write the following words in English letters, and say what the words mean: σκελος, ισος, γωνια, αστρον, γαλα

Exercise 2

In Wordplay you met some ancient words which are used in astronomy.

Make an English adjective from the following ancient words:
luna
sol
orbis
stella
astron
gala
If you are in difficulty, a dictionary may help.

Although you already know some of the adjective suffixes of the words above, there are new ones. Look at lun<u>ar</u>, sol<u>ar</u>, orbit<u>al</u>.

Here are some more adjective suffixes, set out, with examples, according to the sort of sense they give to the word.

al		parental, to do with a parent
ar		popular, to do with the people
ian	("to do with something")	Italian, to do with Italy
an		urban, to do with a town
		(Latin, *urbs* = town)
ary		military, to do with soldiering
		(Latin, *miles* = soldier)
id	("tending to be, like")	timid, tending to be fearful
		(Latin, *timor* = fear)
ous		barbarous, like a monster
ate	("possessing, being")	desperate, being in despair
er	("more")	darker, more dark
est	("most")	darkest, most dark

Exercise 3

Using the suffixes you know, make adjectives out of ten of the incomplete words, and then say what the adjective means. You may use a dictionary.

horizont-	passion-
Mart-	cand-
fortun-	solit-
legend-	regul-
barbar-	Athen-
stup-	tep-
effemin-	famili-
person-	continent-
prim-	compliment-
desol-	second-
frig-	rig-
station-	flu-

A horizont – Mart – feeling solit –.

Exercise 4

Return to the story of Zeus. Pick out any ten adjectives, making sure that you use a variety of suffixes. Underline the suffix, and state what sense it adds to the word.

E.g. monstr<u>ous</u>   like a monster.

Exercise 5

Below you will find a list of adjectives in Latin. They have the Latin adjective suffixes, of which you know the English version. Translate five into English (a dictionary might help), and underline the English adjective suffix.

E.g. *urbanus*   urb<u>an</u>

autumnalis	*destinatus*
obstinatus	*adversarius*
contrarius	*publicus*
Romanus	*humidus*
morbidus	*meridianus*
naturalis	

Unit 5: Hera

1. HERA

Semele was a stunningly beautiful girl, and beauty like hers did
not go unnoticed by Zeus. He saw everything from the snowy
heights of Mount Olympus, but he was particularly attracted to
female beauty. He had had many lovers, and would disguise
5 himself in order to deceive the girls he wanted. He had visited
Europa in the form of a bull, Leda as a swan, and Danae as a
shower of gold wafted into her bedroom on a light breeze. But
none of these could match the beauty of Semele. Zeus loved her,
and soon she was pregnant by him. It was this that made Semele
10 proud.

Hera, wife of Zeus and queen of heaven, was not unmoved by
her husband's infidelity. But it was Semele's display of pride that
she found intolerable. "I could simply strike her down," Hera
thought, "but how much better to let her pride kill her."

15 Hera summoned the clouds and wrapped them around herself.
Thus disguised she descended to earth and changed her
appearance. She spread the fingers of her right hand and drew
deep furrows down her face. These became wrinkles. Her
beautiful hair turned first grey, then white. She put a twist in her
20 spine so that she stooped and walked with difficulty. Her flesh
hung loose on her bones and was almost transparent. Her clothes
were drab and unattractive, her voice unsteady and tremulous, like
that of many old people. When she dismissed the clouds she was
indistinguishable from Semele's nurse.

25 "You're proud of that child you're carrying, aren't you?" she
said to the girl.

"Of course," replied Semele. "It is Zeus' child, and, I
suppose, I'm Zeus' wife. It's a wonderful thing for a girl to be so
loved by the king of the gods." She looked up at her old nurse.
30 She could see that she disapproved of careless talk. Semele
enjoyed that, and provoked the old woman even more. "I
suppose, in a way, that makes me the equal of Hera." Anger
arose in the goddess' heart. She wanted to destroy the girl there
and then, but she would bide her time. Semele saw the old
35 woman's discomfort, and carried on. "If you think about it, Zeus

Hera, queen of heaven

left Hera for me. And he keeps coming back. That makes me better than Hera in Zeus' eyes.''

The old woman interrupted her. "You're talking like a fool. First, you know the gods will never tolerate your arrogance.
40 Secondly, I hope you're sure the father is Zeus. Your reputation would be finished if the child turned out to be imperfect. What if it's weak or deformed? You would never persuade anyone it was the child of Zeus.''

Semele was stung by this. The possibility had never occurred
45 to her. Her lover looked like a mortal, but he had said he was Zeus. She felt as though she were in the presence of a god whenever he visited her. No, the old woman was just being hurtful and unkind.

"Listen, old woman. I know, and you don't." She stood, and
50 then took a few steps towards Hera. "Zeus is my lover. Perhaps you've never had one. I can't imagine any man ever having wanted you." Hera stayed calm. The time for contradicting her was past. Hera would set the trap, and this fool would walk into it.
55 "I knew someone in my youth," said Hera. "A young lad, not a penny to his name. Good looking enough, but I don't think you would fancy him. Anyway, he did all right with the girls. He used to tell them he was a nobleman on a mission for the gods. That often did the trick. Some girls are so gullible." A seed of
60 doubt was planted in Semele's mind.

"Of course," the old woman went on, "a god, even Zeus himself, might take on a human form to win a girl like you. It's happened before. But it's not only gods who have this power. Your lover could equally have been a demon or a monster. Just
65 think, a horrible monster on the inside, the looks of a man outside. It doesn't do to imagine what you have entertained in your bed. Then you must consider what the child of such a thing would be. Painful to you, dishonour to the family. That sort of thing could bring disgrace on the whole city. You know how people talk.''
70 Semele was too angry to rant. Her lips tightened and became thin and colourless. Her knuckles turned white as she clenched her fists. But her voice was calm and her message clear.

"You are a slave. I could have you killed for what you have said to me.'' The old woman was calm too.
75 "I know. But then I'm old. I would only lose a couple of years at the most. At my age, that could be an advantage. No, I was thinking about you. A young girl with a baby and no father to

show for it.   That could be hard.   But if the baby is...not right?
That's not how I would like to live.   You could always...but you're
80 in no mood to listen."

"I could what?"

"I was just thinking.   You could ask your lover to reveal
himself to you as he really is.   You would know soon enough if the
father really is Zeus.   Of course, he would refuse you.   Unless..."

85   The girl was now rushing into the trap.

"Unless," Semele was now speaking Hera's thoughts.
"Unless I ask him to grant me a favour.   Just one.   Then I shall
ask to see him undisguised.   Zeus would have given me his word
and he couldn't go back on it without dishonour."   Semele was as
90 good as dead.

Hera departed for Olympus.   All she had to do now was watch
and wait.   Zeus came to Semele and was eager to embrace her,
but she stopped him: "Would a great god grant his lover a
favour?"

95   "Of course," smiled Zeus.   Hera smiled too.

Unit 5: Hera

"Come to me as Zeus. I want to see you in all your divine glory."

Zeus looked at the girl and shook his head. "I cannot. You don't know what you're asking."

100 "You agreed to one favour. Would almighty Zeus break his word?"

Zeus asked to be freed from this promise. She refused. It must be fulfilled.

Zeus appeared before Semele. Cloud-gatherer, thunderer,
105 wielder of the lightning flash, he glowed with a light more brilliant than any seen on earth. The moment she saw Zeus a surge ran through Semele's bones, like a massive electric shock. The blood began to boil in her veins. Blisters appeared all over her body and she could smell her own flesh being scorched. Her clothes and
110 hair caught fire. Soon the beautiful girl was a scarred mass. Hera's revenge was complete.

Birth of Dionysus

Hermes, the messenger of the gods, saved the baby. It had been in Semele's womb for six months, and was not ready to come into the world. He sewed the baby up in Zeus' thigh so that
115 it could stay safe and warm until the proper time for it to be born. When that time came, the world welcomed a new and mighty god, Dionysus. Because of the miraculous way he came into the world, he was known as "twice born".

Hera was the Queen of Heaven, a daughter of Kronos and Rhea. She came to be seen as goddess of marriage and protector of women in childbirth.

The pomegranate (Latin *pomum granatum*, apple made of seeds) was sacred to her. The seeds in the fruit are seen as a symbol of fertility. Zeus and Hera had many children: the Fates, the Muses, Artemis, Hermes, Ares, Dionysus and Hephaestus. You will hear about most of these.

Exercise 1

1) Why was Hera angry with Zeus?
2) Who did Hera disguise herself as when she visited Semele?
3) What request did Semele make of Zeus?
4) What happened when Zeus granted her wish?

Exercise 2

1) What made Semele's behaviour so bad? Does it matter that she was unaware that she was talking to Hera?
2) What have you learned about Hera that made her a good goddess to protect women?
3) We have said that the gods often behaved and felt as ordinary mortals. Did Hera show any feelings that you think are human?
4) Why should the pomegranate be a good symbol of fertility?
5) Can you think of any reasons why fertility was so important, particularly to people in the ancient world?

2. WORDPLAY

Exercise 1: "I Say No"

Was Zeus kind and caring to Hera?
Was Hera tolerant of Zeus' little ways?
Was Hera concerned for the sad fate of Semele?

Surely the opposite of all these things is true. Zeus was not kind and caring, Hera was not tolerant or concerned. The feelings these gods had were unkind, uncaring, intolerant and unconcerned.

These words all carry a **prefix**.

Write just the prefix for the four words, and then say what that prefix does to the original word.

"Unkind" is the opposite of "kind". "Intolerant" is the opposite of "tolerant". They make the word *negative*, which comes from the Latin *nego*, which means "I say no".

You may know, for instance, that a black and white photograph is printed from a "negative". What is black on the print is white on the negative, and the white on the print is black on the negative. It is the opposite.

SCHOOL REPORT

HARD SUMS : HIS ANSWERS ARE ALWAYS ✗CORRECT

ENGLISH : HIS WORK IS SO ✗TIDY I AM UN✗ABLE TO READ IT.

SCIENCE : HE IS ✗FIT TO BE SET LOOSE IN THE LAB.

NEVER ᵁᴺPUNCTUAL, AND ALWAYS ✗READY FOR WORK. HEAD TEACHER.

UNTOUCHED BY ME, DAD,... HONEST!

TOUCHED BY ME, DAD. DISHONEST!

Exercise 2

Using the prefixes *un* and *in*, write down the words which mean the opposite of these adjectives. That is, make them *negative*:

happy	effective
active	visible
human	hurt
important	

Now do the opposite with the following words. That is, turn them from the negative to the positive, e.g. unmoveable–moveable.

incredible	incorrect
unmoved	unbreakable
unfunny	unfriendly
inescapable	

You can now see how negative words can be built up with the aid of a prefix. The "in" prefix comes from Latin.

Exercise 3

See if you can work out what the following Latin words mean:

incredibilis	*innocens*
interritus	*injustus*
intactus	*inhonoratus*
insanus	*infrequens*
inquietus	*infortunatus*

But it is not only adjectives you can make negative with a prefix.
Look at these examples:

inadvertently	unjustly
uncurl	untruth
untie	inattention
inability	incapacitate
unrest	unpleasantness
inaction	unload

Here are some more prefixes which give a word a negative sense.

Exercise 4: More Negatives

a-, ab-, anti-, dis-, contra-, counter-, mis-, non-, im-.

Using a dictionary, if you want, see how many words you can
find beginning with each prefix. In some cases you will find so
many that you should choose only five or six.

Write down the words you choose and say what they mean.

Exercise 5: Silly Negatives

It is possible to invent some very funny sounding negative words
which can be given a funny meaning. The comedian Ken Dodd
sometimes says that he feels "discumbubulated" when he is
shocked by some news.

If a friend takes a sausage off your plate at school dinner, you
could say that he had "unsausagified" you.

Can you invent some odd-sounding negative adjectives? Say
what you think they should mean.

DISTROUSERATED

Exercise 6

Go through the story of Hera again, and list ten words you can
find made negative by a prefix. Say what the word means. You
may use a dictionary.

3. GRAMMAR

Exercise 1: Latin and Greek Negatives

Here are some negative words in Latin and Greek. See if you can
work out what they mean. A dictionary will help you if you get
stuck. For instance, if I gave you the Latin word *immaturus*, you
would find its English form under "immature". This will not help
you in every case, though.

controversia δυσπεπτος
discors αντιδοτος
immoderatus αθεος
dissimilis αντιθεσις
indefensus

The Word That Does Things

You now know about nouns and adjectives, and the job they do
in a sentence. Another sort of word you must know about is the
verb.

It is a word of **action** or **doing**, **being** or **being done**.
I **do** my exercises.
I **fly** gliders.
I **am** a flier.
I **am being flown** home in a helicopter.
You will see as you read that most sentences have a verb.

Any action that happens must happen at some time or other.
For instance:

On Christmas Eve you might say: "Tomorrow **I shall open** my
presents."
On Christmas Day: "**I am opening** my presents."
On Boxing Day: "Yesterday **I opened** my presents."
These sentences show you the three main times a verb can
happen: the future, the present (now), or the past time.

If a verb describes an action yet to happen, the verb is in the
future tense.
If the action is happening now, it is in the **present tense**.
If the action has already happened, it is in the **past tense**.

FUTURE

ROCKET WILL
DETONATE
IN FIVE SECONDS

PRESENT

ROCKET
IS
DETONATING

PAST

ROCKET
HAS DETONATED
SUCCESSFULLY

Exercise 2

Pick out the verbs in the following sentences, and then say what
the tenses are: present, future or past.

"You made the mess. You will clear it up because it is making
the floor slippy."

The teacher is walking *along the*   *The teacher* has slipped *in the mess*   *The teacher* will be angry *with*
corridor   *someone*

If a verb is a word of "doing", then someone or something must
do it, or have it done to them. That someone or something is called
the person of the verb.

If there is only one person, it will be **I, you, he, she, it**, or some
thing.

If there is more than one person, it will be **we, you, they**, or
some things.

So let's write out all the present tense to the verb "to slip":

Singular (i.e. one person or thing does it)

I slip
You slip
He, she, it slips

Plural (more than one)

We slip
You slip
They slip

Exercise 3

Write out the future and past tenses of the verb "to slip". Copy the pattern given above. Here is a start:

Future   Past

I will slip   I slipped
You . . .   You . . .
etc.   etc.

We also refer to the **person** of the verb. The **first person** is the speaker, **I**; the **second person** is the one spoken to, **you**. The **third person** is the one spoken about, **he** or **she**.

In the plural, the first person is **we**, the second person is **you**, the third person is **they**.

Exercise 4

Pick out the verbs from the following and write their **tense** and **person** and state whether the person is singular or plural.

E.g. Harry (i.e. he) skated too fast — Verb: skated; Person: 3rd singular; Tense: past

We shall be late — Verb: shall be; Person: 1st (plural); Tense: future

Try the same with this passage:

"I am sick and tired of hearing what you have done. Your parents will hear about this. And your father is a good friend of mine. You will not get away with it this time."

Finally:

Exercise 5:

Find ten verbs in the story about Hera. Write the verb down and state its tense and person, singular or plural.

Unit 6: Demeter

1. DEMETER

Without a sound the ghosts approached Hades' throne. Some stretched their arms out to him in an appeal for help. Others anxiously raised their eyes to the roof of Hell above them. A distinct tremor could be felt, and now and then a trickle of dust
5 descended to dirty the hair or irritate the eyes of the joyless people of the dark kingdom beneath the earth. But should a crack appear and let light into Hell the ghosts would have to scatter and hide. The bright sun in heaven gives light, warmth and life to the earth, but it is not welcome to the souls of the dead. They feel secure in
10 the dark damp chill of the Underworld.

Hades was kind to his people. They invoked his help, and he spoke kindly to them.

"There is no need to worry. The Titans that Zeus buried are struggling to get out. They cannot do that, but every now and then
15 they do set the earth shaking a little. I shall go above and see that there are no cracks in the earth's surface which might let in the light."

The ghosts nodded silently in thanks. Some may have been moved to smile, but instead turned away content that their king
20 would protect them. There is no smiling in Hell.

Erebus is the passage to the Underworld. Its mouth stands by a lake and this is where Hades leaves one world for another.

The god is approaching the world of light. The rumble in the earth becomes visible as the lake's surface breaks into ripples
25 which move from the mouth of Erebus to the shores around it. The sound increases and the ripples turn into waves. The rumble becomes a roar from the depths of Hell, and the cold breeze issuing from Erebus is soon an icy blast as Hades breaks out in his black chariot drawn by four horses only he can control.
30 Such is the speed of the vehicle that as it emerges from Hell it leaves the earth for a few seconds. The deafening roar ceases immediately. Silence. The horses draw the chariot up into the air and then descend in a perfect arc. The leading horses take the impact as they hit the earth. The next two follow close behind,
35 bringing the chariot to earth with a clap like thunder. Then there is just the cloud of dust as the chariot speeds to its destination.

Hades was soon content that the earth had suffered no damage
from the recent disturbances. He wheeled the horses round and
began to head back for Erebus. But a sudden deep pain in his
40 chest made him stagger. He reined in the horses and the vehicle
came to a stop. His hand went to his chest and the clothing felt
damp. As he looked down he saw an arrow shaft and the brightly
coloured flights. He had been shot in the heart. Gods cannot die,
and their veins carry not blood but the holy ichor. But the wound
45 did hurt, and more so as he dragged the barbed head from deep
within his chest. He pressed the wound together to close it, and
then drove on.

Aphrodite, goddess of love, had watched all this from the
snowy heights of Olympus. It was her son Eros who had fired the
50 arrow into Hades' heart and filled him with desire. "After all,"
Aphrodite thought to herself, "poor old Hades must be very lonely
down there in the Underworld with only the ghosts for company.
What he needs is a good woman to take his mind off things. He
will fall for the girl he sets eyes on next."

55 Persephone was in a field picking wild flowers. She liked to
take them to her mother, and Demeter was happy to receive them.

Hades saw Persephone from a distance. Being full of
Aphrodite's poison, he found any female form provocative.
Persephone was truly beautiful. He reined in his horses to
60 walking pace and slowly approached the girl. She turned as he
approached, and then stood, flowers in one hand, the other
shading her eyes from the bright sun. The light breeze moved the
fine fabric of her dress over her body, and Hades' heart leapt.

Persephone had no reason to fear any man, although the
65 appearance of Hades, tall in his black chariot, was disturbing even
to her. Hades pulled the chariot beside her. She tilted her
beautiful head and smiled politely, expecting to be spoken to. But
Hades had nothing to say. He grabbed the girl by the arm and
pulled her towards him. She tried to shake him off, but did not
70 have the strength. Hades put his other arm round her waist,
hoisted her off the ground and swung her into the chariot beside
him. She thrust her elbows into his chest, trying to separate
herself from him. Terror was in her eyes as she shook her head.
She pleaded. Hades paid no attention. She struggled more. She
75 panicked. "Let me go!"

She then thought of her mother and called to her for help. But
Demeter was not around. Hades whipped his horses to a gallop,
and as he approached the lake he dropped the reins, picked up his

Demeter

sceptre, and threw it into the water. The way to Hell opened up in
80 the waters, and Persephone's vociferous complaints were silenced
as they entered the cold dark world of the dead.

When Persephone failed to return home, Demeter went out
looking for her. The girl was nowhere to be found, and no one
had seen her. Demeter continued her search, but she knew in her
85 heart the longer she searched, the less likely she was to find her.
Passing the lake at Hell's entrance, Demeter saw something
floating on the surface. She took a stick and fished it out. It was
the belt Persephone had been wearing the morning she left to pick
flowers.

90 Demeter feared the worst, and turned her sorrow and anger on
the very land Persephone had left.

Demeter was the goddess who made all plants, flowers and
crops grow. But in her anger she decided to abandon her
responsibilities. Earth that had been fertile and productive now
95 stopped growing anything. The green and fruitful landscape soon
looked like a bare, barren rock. As she mourned the loss of
Persephone, the people grew hungry.

She returned to the lake where she had found the belt. She
gazed into the water as though she might see where her daughter
100 was. As she peered into the waters, a beautiful young girl
emerged. The nymph stood shoulder deep in the water, her
beautiful hair, all wet, clinging to her.

"I saw your daughter as she left this land. She is safe, but
imprisoned in Hell with the souls of the dead. Hades fell in love
105 with her and took her to his kingdom to be his queen. You should
not blame the land for this. Your sorrow is great, but that is no
reason to kill off the human race."

The girl finished speaking, smiled, and disappeared beneath
the water again. Demeter immediately went to Olympus to plead
110 with Zeus.

Zeus felt pity. He had loved Demeter, and Persephone was
his own cherished daughter. "There is one thing you must
understand," he said. "I can bring Persephone back from the
Underworld only if she has eaten nothing in that kingdom. If she
115 has eaten, Fate decrees that she must stay, and there is nothing
that even I, king of the gods, can do to overturn that.

Meanwhile, Persephone was pining in the Underworld. She
was cold and lonely. She missed the warmth of the sun, the
flowers and trees and the company of her mother. The ghosts
120 were silent and gloomy. None was happy there, and the sadness

Persephone

only reminded her of the joy of her past life.

Hades did all he could to cheer her up. He loved her and wanted to make her happy, but Persephone had shut him out of her heart. She wandered about in the dark kingdom chewing the
125 last of the six pomegranate seeds which had been her only food since she had been seized.

Zeus broke the news to Demeter. Only six seeds, but Fate was adamant, and the girl was doomed to eternity in the dark kingdom.

130   Demeter returned to earth. She wandered around wrapped up in her grief. At last she was tired and found a rock to sit on. She drew her knees to her chin, folded her arms round her legs, and, swaying gently back and forth, moaned to herself of her sadness. And the land grew colder and more lifeless as she mourned.

135   Zeus saw the disaster which had hit the land and the people who lived there. He wanted to act, but could not oppose Fate. Nevertheless, he might find a compromise that would suit all.

Zeus explained in detail to Hades what had happened since he had taken Persephone into his kingdom. Hades nodded, but said
140 he would not give up Persephone. With a wide sweep of his arms, he addressed the king of the gods. "Look around you. This was the kingdom I was allotted when you took power over heaven and Poseidon was granted the seas. It is a lonely place and you don't hear laughter from the poor souls who live here. I know they need
145 me, and I am satisfied that my vocation is to be their just ruler. But I love Persephone. She is the only beautiful thing here, and even her sadness is a beacon of joy in this land of the dead. She is the only one who can touch my soul and make me smile."

Zeus understood his brother and sympathised. The two great
150 gods agreed on a plan which would save the earth and not offend Fate. For each pomegranate seed Persephone had eaten she would stay a month each year in Hades. The other six months she could spend with Demeter on the earth, provided she return to Hades again.

155   The compromise was good. Each spring Persephone returned to Demeter. The land came alive and the seeds in it stirred and started to grow. In the heat of the summer the crops ripened and the earth was rich. But in autumn, Persephone returned to Hades. Demeter's grief came back. The land slowly died off and people
160 had to harvest what it had produced in the summer. By winter the earth was dead. Demeter's land was a land of death, just like

Persephone's. But life would return. The newly invented seasons
would continue their cycle forever.

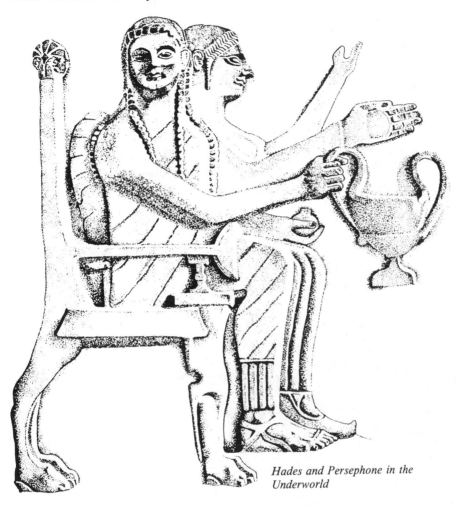

*Hades and Persephone in the
Underworld*

Exercise 1

1)   Why did Hades leave the Underworld in the first place?
2)   What made Hades fall so desperately in love?
3)   What did Demeter find to convince her that her daughter was
lost?
4)   What was so bad about the fact that Demeter went into
mourning?
5)   Why could Zeus not free Persephone from the Underworld?
6)   How was the problem of the earth not producing anything
solved?

Exercise 2

1) Why should a goddess who makes things grow be so important to the Greeks? Can you think of any countries where she might not be important?

2) You know that the gods are very different from ordinary mortal people. But can you find any examples in the story of gods feeling and behaving just like mortals?

3) Can you think of any other religious stories in which someone returns from the land of the dead to the land of the living?

4) How good was the compromise reached at the end of the story? Did anyone end up completely happy? Was there any other way around this problem?

5) Is there a villain in this story or not? If you think there is, who is it, and what did he or she do wrong?

2. WORDPLAY

Exercise 1: Words Which Have a Voice

Return to the story and look at lines 11, 58, 80 and 145.

Read them aloud and try to find a group of words which have something in common. Is there a sound or group of letters they share? The list includes "provocative", "invoked", "vociferous" and "vocation".

The fact that the same sound or a similar group of letters occurs might mean that the words have a similar meaning.

Look up these words in your dictionary, and write the definitions. Just one short definition will do. Now look at what you have, and see if you can find one idea contained in all these words.

If you have a vocabulary book do you know *exactly* what it is? Look up the word "vocabulary".

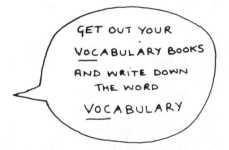

Vok or *voc*, which occurs in all these words, comes from the Latin word *vox*, which means "voice" and *vocare*, "to call". For instance, for "invoke" you may have the definition "to call upon". It means that because the *vok* part comes from the Latin for "voice". Look at the other words and work out why the *voc*, *vok* part is there.

This part of the word is called the **root**, because it forms the basis of the word's meaning. But you can add to the beginning and end of it to give even more meaning.

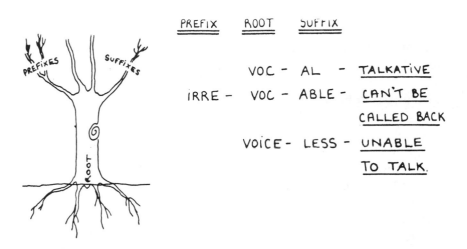

PREFIX   ROOT   SUFFIX

VOC - AL - TALKATIVE

IRRE - VOC - ABLE - CAN'T BE
CALLED BACK

VOICE - LESS - UNABLE
TO TALK.

Exercise 2: "Get the Phone"

The Greek form of *vox* is *phone*. So all the following words have a "voice" sense in common.

telephone	symphony
microphone	Anglophone
megaphone	Francophone
saxophone	xylophone
phonetic	

Choose any four words from the list. Explain why each of your words should contain the idea of "voice".

Again, knowing the root word might tell you something you did not realise before. For instance, a saxophone is a musical instrument. You know the "-phone" part, but the prefix refers to the man who invented the instrument. What do you think his name was?

What do you think Mr. Sousa called his invention?

Most of the words in the "-phone" list have a **prefix**: a group of letters which come *before* "phone" (a **suffix** would be a group of letters *following* phone).

INVENTED A MUSICAL INSTRUMENT, MR SOUSA?

Exercise 3

Split the following words into **prefix** and "-phone/phony".
    telephone
    microphone
    megaphone
    symphony
Find another word which has the same prefix as each of these. For example, from "telephone" you might think of "telescope".

The prefix will add some meaning to the root "phone".

Exercise 4

The following list of words all have the same prefix:

microphone	microorganism
microscope	microbe
microchip	microfilm
microsurgery	microbiology

If you don't know any of these words look them up. See if, from what they mean, you can work out the sense of the prefix "micro".

You can then do the same with the prefixes "tele-", "mega-", and "sym-".

Words like this are simply built up, like "lego" bricks, of bits that have their own meaning. Put the bits together, and you get the meaning of the whole word.

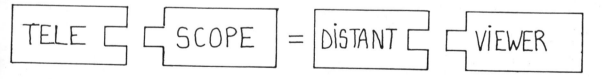

Exercise 5

If an Anglophone is someone who speaks English, what are the following? A dictionary will again give you some help:

    Francophone   Hispanophone   Italophone   Sinophone

Exercise 6: Inventaword

Using your ancient word list, build up some "phone" words of your own. They don't need to exist, but you can define what they ought to mean if they did. For instance:

  agora means "market place". An "agoraphone" might be a market trader who is good at the salesman's "spiel".

Jocosus means funny or joking. Punch could be called "jocoso-phone".

When you have invented some "phone" words, challenge your friends to define them.

3. GRAMMAR

Exercise 1: Using the Greek Alphabet

Look at the following Greek words with their meanings. Try to say them aloud and then write them out in English letters so that if an English person read them they could get as close as possible to the Greek sound.

e.g	φωνασκεω	I learn to sing	*phonaskeo*
	φωνεω	I speak	
	φωνομιμος	imitating the voice	
	φωνομαχια	a quarrel about words	

The English version of these words is called "phonetic" because you have written them exactly as they sound. In some dictionaries you are shown how a word is pronounced by being given the phonetic form of the word. For instance, Chambers's dictionary has this entry:

  exercise, *eks er sīz*

eks er siz 2

What words do you think the following phonetic forms represent?

  jēog ra fi

  sī ens

  lan gwij

Here are three English words, following by their phonetic spelling:

trough	trof
women	wimmin
nation	nayshun

There is an old trick you can play with these letters and sounds. Pronounce the following word: "ghoti".

Take *gh* as in "trough", *o* as in "women", and *ti* as in "nation", and you get "fish".

This, though, is only a joke. The phonetic spelling of "fish" is, simply, *fish*!

Again we have been looking at words which are built up from two or more parts, as, for instance, xylo-phone. *Xylon* is the Greek for "wood", and the instrument is "wood voiced" because the sounding blocks of the xylophone are made of wood.

You know what a noun is, and you know what a prefix is. Here is a noun, which has a prefix. Can you separate off the prefix? The word is **pronoun**.

The prefix *pro* is a Latin word which means "instead of". Our new part of speech is the **pronoun**, which you already know, simply by looking at the word, means "an instead-of-a-noun".

Look at the following passage:

Teacher was shopping on Saturday morning and teacher saw Janet. Janet said "Good morning, teacher" and teacher replied "Good morning Janet. What is Janet shopping for?" "Janet is shopping for clothes for Janet," replied Janet. "Well," replied teacher, "Teacher hopes that Janet gets what Janet wants."

Is this how you or your friends speak?

Exercise 3

Rewrite the passage, changing anything in the language which does not feel right to you. Try to end up with a piece of natural sounding English.

MENU

GHOTI KĀKS WITH

PĒZ OR BĒNZ

What you have probably done is changed the nouns for shorter forms. "Teacher" might become "he" or "she". "Janet" might become "she" or "her" and so on. For instance, the last sentence might read "Well," he replied, "I hope you get what you want." So wherever you have put a word instead of a noun, you have written a **pronoun**. They will, of course, be words like: him, her, them, he, she, me, you, we, this, that etc.

Exercise 4

Read through the story of Demeter again. Pick out 15 pronouns, and then say what noun you think they are replacing. Give the line number for the pronoun you are dealing with. E.g.:

line 1: some stretched their arms out to him in an appeal for help. "Him" stands for "Hades".

Exercise 5

Pick out pronouns from the following tunes.

IT'S THE RIGHT ONE,
IT'S THE BRIGHT ONE,
IT'S MARTINI.

I LOVE YOU AND YOU LOVE ME
OH MY DARLING CAN'T YOU SEE...?

MAYBE IT'S BECAUSE I'M A LONDONER
THAT I LOVE LONDON SO..
MAYBE IT'S BECAUSE I'M A LONDONER
THAT I THINK OF HER
WHEREVER I GO....

TETLEY BITTERMEN

IF YOU CAN'T BEAT 'EM
JOIN 'EM.

There is also another kind of pronoun which you will meet regularly. Look at the following examples:

That is the boy <u>who</u> hit me.

This is the subject <u>which</u> I like best.

Where is the book <u>that</u> I was reading?

The words underlined are all pronouns. The first stands for "boy", the second for "subject", the third for "book". These also help to link two parts of the sentence. "That is the boy. The boy hit me" has been made into one sentence by using "who". It is a word which links or relates things. And that is why words like *who, which, what, that* etc. are called **relative pronouns**.

Exercise 6

Make the following pairs of sentences one by using a relative pronoun.

This is the teacher. I like the teacher.

I have read that book. It is the best book.

Where is the dog. I lost it.

This is the problem. I can't solve the problem.

"WHICH" IS THE RELATIVE PRONOUN "THAT" I LOVE BEST.

Unit 7: Apollo

1. APOLLO

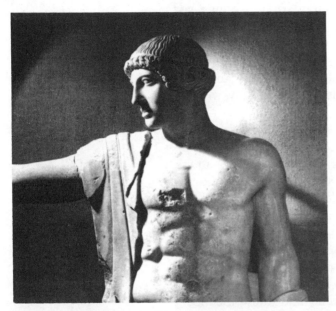

The earth was waterlogged. Zeus and Poseidon had unleashed all the waters of heaven and earth to destroy the human race because of its wickedness, but two innocent mortals had been preserved to start a new and better race.

5 Now, however, the storm clouds were clearing and the sun was shining on the earth for the first time in weeks. Gradually the earth dried and the sun's heat penetrated deep into it and warmed the seeds which the gods had left there. Some of these would come to life, others remain dormant. Some seeds would develop
10 into plants and animals. Some would be monsters never seen before on the earth.

 One such seed had come to life in the earth. Tons of caked mud lay above it, but it grew so quickly that deep cracks soon appeared in the mud. A huge scaly body began to writhe in the
15 earth in a desperate attempt to break out of its grave. The heartbeat grew stronger, driving cold blood to all parts of the snake's body.

 The head was the first to emerge from the earth. It was huge,

flat across the top with bulging eyes on each side of it. A long
20 forked tongue flickered in and out of its mouth which had two
great fangs at the front. The monster opened its mouth wide
gulping in the air it couldn't get beneath the earth. Its gape was so
huge that it looked like a deep red gash as big as the mouth of a
cave. Its body was all muscle, and it thrust itself out of the earth
25 straight towards heaven in its search for air. Now towering over
the landscape, the snake was content that it could breathe.

Slowly, carefully, it drew itself back down to the ground and
dragged the whole vast length of its body out of the earth. Tired
from all this effort, it slithered to a hillside to survey the land
around. Its green scaly body covered the hill completely with its
30 coils.

It slept for a while, and then made off in search of food. Its
attack was sudden, silent and deadly. It could account for a whole
flock of sheep in a single foray, and it was prepared to attack
35 people too. Those who lived in the area soon learned to fear it,
because they were helpless against its hideous strength.

Zeus was aware of what was happening to these people who
lived around Delphi, and sent Apollo, god of archery, to consider
the situation. He never went without his bow and arrows, and
40 Zeus knew that he was the best to deal with the monster if he had
to.

Apollo saw destruction all around him, and knew the beast
must die. He carefully considered the land around the hillside and
chose the best spot for his assault. He crouched and surveyed his
45 target. It had just eaten. He could see blood around its jaws; its
huge, coiled body was relaxed. The eyes were open, but glazed.
Perhaps it was asleep. Could he kill it with one arrow? If not,
what sort of fight would he have to face when it was wounded and
angry?
50 Apollo stood up. He reached for an arrow from his quiver and
fitted the notched end onto the bowstring. He half drew the bow
before raising his left arm to level the point of the arrow in the
direction of the snake. He locked his elbow and smoothly drew
the arrow back to his right ear. He could feel the bowstring and
55 the feathered flight on his cheek. The shot was to be a long one
and a slight breeze blew from left to right. He compensated by
directing the aim slightly to the left above the head of the beast,
took a deep breath, and held it. His right hand freed the
bowstring. The bow straightened and sent the arrow fast into the
60 air.

Apollo lowered the bow and watched the arrow's flight. It reached its highest point and dropped slightly. The breeze carried it to the right. The beast did not move. The barbed head of the arrow burst into the neck immediately beneath the snake's head.
65 The scales offered some resistance, but not enough. The shaft was buried two, three inches into the flesh which opened up to display a deep wound, red against the green background of the scales of its neck. At first the creature looked stunned, but showed no pain. It did not even know what had woken it. But the
70 second arrow that buried itself beneath the first sent a shock of agony through its whole body.

The third and fourth arrows opened up the wound even more. Blood now gushed out with force, like a river breaking through a dam which can no longer hold the water back. The earth beneath
75 became sodden. Then the blood became darker as the poison the snake used on its victims found its way out of the same wound. The earth which had given the monster birth was wet again, this time not with water, but with blood and poison.

Five, six, seven arrows had now reached their mark. The
80 snake, though weakened, was still powerful. It gathered its strength and was poised to strike. It spied its attacker, bared the teeth which still carried venom, and lunged at Apollo. He stood his ground, still firing and still hitting his mark with every arrow. The snake's head, now within feet of the god, tilted back so that
85 the fangs were directed at his face, but the final, forward thrust was never completed. The monster relaxed as the blood and poison continued to flow and the muscles in its body went loose.

For a moment it supported its own weight and stayed hovering above Apollo. Then gently, not with any cry of agony, with no
90 lashing of the tail or writhing of the body, it sank to earth as though tired and wanting to sleep. Apollo checked the quiver. He had fired all his arrows and saved the people of Delphi.

This great snake, called Python, had also served the gods in its life. It had protected the oracle at Delphi - a place where people
95 could go and ask about the future. Apollo would not deprive people of such an opportunity, so he adopted the oracle himself and appointed a priestess who could convey to mortals the answers the gods gave to their questions. In honour of the monster, and also to keep alive the memory of his great victory,
100 Apollo named her Pythia.

Apollo, like many other gods, fell in love with a mortal girl. But Cassandra would not give in to him unless he gave her something in return. She promised that she would become his lover if he taught her to see and interpret the future. Apollo
105 agreed and set about teaching her all she needed to know about discovering what was to happen.

Once she had gained all the knowledge she needed she went back on her word and refused to have anything to do with the the god. Apollo was angry at having been tricked by the girl, and
110 wanted to punish her. But he knew he couldn't take away the knowledge she already had. Then he came across the perfect solution to his problem. Cassandra must keep the knowledge she had, but he could make it useless to her. It was her fate always to speak the truth but never to be believed. All the power she had
115 through knowing the future was worth nothing.

The gods knew that knowledge of the future would not always be good for mortals. How happy would you be if you knew that you, or someone you loved, was fated to suffer some terrible disaster? The gods also knew that knowledge of this sort might
120 make people too powerful and lead them to disrespect the gods. So the answers to requests for knowledge were not always clear. They were ambiguous and could be interpreted more than one way. Sometimes the answers, though quite true, were actually misleading.
125 Like the other gods, Apollo had several particular abilities. As a musician he could play beautifully and inspire people to do so. His favourite instrument was the lyre, a stringed instrument like a small harp which had, as a sound box, a turtle shell.

It might be difficult to fully understand the importance of

130 music to the Greeks: it was required for religious festivals, and for
the dancing and singing which were a part of them. Closely
connected were the singing and reciting of poetry which was the
form of story telling most commonly used to speak of the gods and
men who had made the Greeks what they were.

Exercise 1

1)   How did the gods decide to destroy the human race?
2)   How was the human race made again after the destruction?
3)   Who killed Python, and how?
4)   Why did Delphi become so famous?
5)   How did Apollo show some respect for Python?

Exercise 2

1)   List three special abilities of Apollo. Why should the Greeks
see these as important to themselves? Which of his skills would
you most like to have? Why?
2)   How many instruments can you think of which work like a
lyre?
3)   What events can you think of which involve music, singing or
dancing? Why do you think people play, sing or dance at such
events?
4)   If you could ask the oracle one question about the future,
what would it be? Why would you want to know that?
5)   What methods do people use nowadays to try to find out the
future?

2. WORDPLAY

"Any Future You Want"

You know that an oracle was a place where people could ask a
god about the future. You have also been told that the answers
were not always clear. Often one statement about the future
could be taken in two ways.

For instance, King Croesus once asked the oracle if he should
make war on his enemy. The reply was: "If you cross the river,
you will destroy a great army."

Imagine you are Croesus, and you had just received that

oracle. Would you cross the river and fight?

If your answer is "yes", you might feel cheated to discover that you lost the battle and destroyed your own army! But the oracle had still told the truth.

Nero was told by the oracle to "fear the 73rd year". Happy in the prospect of a good, long life, imagine how cheated he felt being killed by the 73-year-old Galba.

Exercise 1: "Say What You Mean"

The Latin word *ambiguus* means "going in two directions"; the English "ambiguous" means "of doubtful meaning". Latin *ambi-* = Greek *amphi-*, meaning "both", "on both sides", and sometimes "around".

Look at the cartoons and say what is ambiguous about each of the statements. Can you think of any instructions given by a teacher which could be ambiguous?

Unit 7: Apollo

What name do we give to an animal which has both lungs and gills so that it can breathe under water and in the air? Clue: remember the Greek word *bios*. (The answer is at the bottom of the page.)

Exercise 2

Look up the following words (if you need to). Write down the definition and then explain the use of the *ambi-, amphi-* prefix.

ambidextrous
amphitheatre
amphipod
amphora

THANKYOU FOR THE HOMEWORK.
I SHALL WASTE NO TIME IN MARKING IT!

Telling the future could be called "supernatural". Write a sentence including the word "supernatural" showing that you understand what the word means.

Exercise 3

Write three words beginning with the prefix "super-", and see if you can work out what the prefix means from those words. Look to see if they have any meaning in common.

    See below for answer.

Exercise 4

Here is a list of words with the prefix "super-". Say what they mean. Before looking any up, try to guess from the prefix.

superman	superexcellent
supergirl	superfluous
supersonic	superintend
superimpose	superior
supervise	supertax
superhuman	supercallifragilisticexpialidocious

Inventaword

"Ambi", "amphi" and "super" are good prefixes for word invention. Using your ancient words list invent and define some new things. They can be weird as you like. On the next page are some to start with:

"Super" means "above".   The answer is "amphibion".

ambimagisterial: describes someone who teaches two subjects, or perhaps two classes.
amphikitharistes: someone who can play two harps at once.
ambiminister: a double agent
supercapital: a ball the goalie can't reach
superambilocution: talking over someone while going round
the topic.

3. GRAMMAR

Exercise 1: Using the Greek Alphabet

Here are some words in Greek and Latin with the "amphi"/
"ambi" prefix. Write out the Greek in English letters, and then
see if you can work out what the Latin and Greek words mean.
You may use a dictionary.

αμφιβιος   *ambitio*
αμφιδεξιος   *ambiguitas*
αμφιθεατρον   *ambitus*
αμφορευς

Here are some Greek words in English letters, with their meanings. Write them in Greek letters:

amphibainō   I go around
amphithalassos   with sea on both sides
amphikephalos   with two heads
amphinoeō   I am in two minds, unsure

You now know the following parts of speech: **noun, adjective,
pronoun, verb**.

An adjective describes a noun, as in "How now, <u>brown</u> cow."
But what if you want to describe *how* something is done? That is,
if you want to describe the verb? "The brown cow mooed
quietly". "Quietly" tells you how the cow mooed, and so it
describes the verb. Any word which does this is called an **adverb**.
Adverbs in English often end in -ly, but not always.

Exercise 2

Write five adverbs for the way a cow might moo.

Adverbs can also tell you more about an adjective, e.g. the music is
incredibly loud.

Again, find five more adverbs which tell how loud the music was.

Finally, an adverb can also describe another adverb:

   I acted <u>terribly</u> bravely.

Again, five more, please, to describe how bravely.

There are many adverbs which do not end in -ly. Here are some: well, late, likewise, fast, enough, soon. You can check this by seeing how they can all describe a verb: "You have done well and worked late."

Exercise 3

Take the adverbs "likewise, fast, enough, soon" and write a sentence or some sentences to show how they can describe a verb (or an adjective, or an adverb).

Exercise 4

Return to the Apollo story. Pick out any eight adverbs and state which word they describe. Then say whether that word is a verb, an adjective or an adverb.

Just as you can often tell an English adverb by the suffix -ly, so you can tell a Latin or Greek one by its suffix.

   The commonest suffixes for Latin adverbs are *-e* and *-iter* (or *-ter*, or *-er*). In Greek the commonest is -ως.

Exercise 5

See if you can work out what the following Greek and Latin
adverbs mean:

Latin	Greek
similiter	φανταστιχως
difficulter	τεχνιχως
constanter	λογιχως
ridicule	αριθμητιχως
miserabile	πραχτιχως

Unit 8: Artemis

1. ARTEMIS

In the woods the ground was wet, stained with the blood of wild animals. Actaeon and his friends had had a good morning's hunting, but midday was coming on fast.

5 In Greece the afternoon sun is not kind to those who are out hunting. It scorches the earth and cruelly saps men of their strength. It was time to have a rest. The young men stacked their spears together and looked for some shade to lie in for a while.

The goddess Artemis had also been out hunting. She, too, was hot and tired and midday was her hour for the bath. In the
10 depths of the wood there was a cave at the foot of a cliff and there in the coolness and shade the fresh water fell into a clear pool in the rock, and there was Artemis, attended, as always, by her nymphs. Their duties were to prepare the goddess for the bath. They saw to her bow and arrows and quiver. They removed her
15 clothing and cared for it and then they were ready to join her at her bath, pouring water over her divine body and afterwards playing with her in the pool.

This was a secret cave deep in the forest. Artemis was the virgin goddess and the guardian of unmarried girls. It was
20 unthinkable that a man should set eyes on her naked body.

Actaeon's friends had all fallen asleep, but Actaeon was restless and had gone walking in the woods. As he wandered aimlessly along the river banks and through the trees, he suddenly came to a cliff face and from deep in the green shade of it heard
25 strange sounds. Was that splashing? Was that laughter? Was it human? Without an evil thought in his mind, he climbed over the rocks and stood at the entrance to the cave and looked in.

The laughter stopped. There stood the goddess in all her
naked beauty, taller than all her nymphs. And there was Actaeon
30 looking at her. The nymphs screamed and tried to cover their
nakedness and at the same time to hide the body of the goddess.
But Actaeon had seen the goddess and the goddess knew that he
had seen.

We would feel sympathy for Actaeon. He had gone there
35 quite innocently but by a combination of circumstances he had
done something that the goddess could not accept and could not
condone. That a man should see the naked body of the virgin
goddess was not compatible with her divinity, and certainly not
compatible with her virginity.

40 Punishment was swift and decisive and it surprised Actaeon.
The goddess sprinkled him with water and said, "Now go and tell
your friends that you have seen the naked body of the virgin
Artemis."

Actaeon felt strange. A ripple in the water made it look as
45 though something was growing from his forehead. He checked
again. His neck had lengthened, his ears were becoming pointed
and he was growing horns. His hands contracted to become
hooves, split down the middle. His skin now felt like fur.
Bewilderment turned to panic, and in his panic he ran.

50 But he had never run like this before. He was on all fours, and
his long legs took him faster than he had ever travelled. He also
noticed that everything frightened him. The lightest rustle of the
undergrowth caused him to pause and look around. He felt timid
and threatened, as though in danger.

55 Though he looked like a deer, there was still enough of the
human in him to consider his situation. Contact his friends. They
would see him safe. He tried to call for help but no recognisable
syllables emerged. He wept, and huge tears coursed down his
snout and struck the ground like great drops of blood. Where
60 could he go? His appearance excluded him from human society,
his mind from that of animals.

The pack of hounds had caught his scent. They knew what to
do. They had been well trained by their master Actaeon. They
swept over the rocky terrain, through hollows and down cliffs.

65 Actaeon's experience as a huntsman led him to those parts
where he knew deer had the best chance of survival. He tried
calling to the hounds: "I am Actaeon. You know me!" But they
did not know him.

The first hound went for his neck, while two more brought him

70 down by the shoulders. They held him long enough for the rest of
the pack to arrive. They tore the beast apart, just as Actaeon had
taught them. Next came his friends. They cheered on the hounds
eagerly as they looked for their leader.

"Actaeon will be sorry to have missed this. Where on earth is
75 he?" With one final effort, Actaeon raised himself to his knees.
Silently he turned his head. His antlers were like arms stretched
out in prayer. The final death cry was unlike anything the hunters
had heard before. It filled the forest and lived in their minds
forever.

Exercise 1

1) Why were Actaeon and his friends in the wood?
2) What time of day was it?
3) What did Actaeon discover while wandering?
4) Why should he not have seen what he did?
5) Say, very briefly, how he died.

We know that Artemis was a huntress, but she was also the
protector of wild animals. She was the goddess who looked after
young unmarried girls, and at the same time the guardian of
women in childbirth. This was because she helped her mother
Leto deliver Apollo, her twin brother who was born after her.

Exercise 2

1) What do we learn of the character of the goddess from this story?

2) Why do you think Artemis killed Actaeon in the way that she did? Was there any justice in this?

3) Why should the ancients acknowledge a goddess of a function as natural as childbirth?

4) Huntress and protector of animals, virgin goddess and helper of women in childbirth, Artemis might seem to have charge over things that are apparent opposites. Can you see any sense in the system?

5) Look at the picture and the one on p.81. How have the artists departed from the story of Actaeon's death? Why do you think they have represented it in this way?

2. WORDPLAY

Actaeon died in the presence of his companions. He remained conscious throughout the ordeal knowing that he could not contact his friends.

You may have noticed the use of the prefixes "con-", "com-". These come from the Latin *cum* and mean "together, with". The Greek *sym*, *syn* (sometimes *syl*) has the same force at the beginning of a word.

Here are some examples of English words with that prefix:
sympathy: Greek *sym* + Greek *pathos* (feeling, suffering): feeling with
synthetic: Greek *syn* + Greek *thesis* (putting): put together
compel: Latin *com* + Latin *pello* (I drive, force): force together
concord: Latin *con* + Latin *cor* (heart): together in heart

CONCORD   CONCORDE

C'EST BON   JOLLY GOOD

Exercise 1

Look through the story of Artemis and Actaeon. Find five words prefixed with any of the parts given above (con-, com-, sym-, syn-, syl-). Write the word down, underline the prefix, look up the meaning and then explain the job the prefix is doing.

E.g. if you found the word "constant", you would write:
constant: fixed, standing firm or together.   "Con" means "together".

Exercise 2

In column 1 you will find a Latin word with its meaning. Combine
this with the prefix con-, com- to make an English word. You will
see other forms of the Latin word in brackets. These will help you
find the English word you want. The meaning of the English word
is also given to help you. Just complete the last column. The first
two are completed to show you how it's done.

Latin	Prefix	Meaning	English
claudo (clud, clus) I shut	con	shut together, close	conclude
coquo (coct) I cook	con	cook together, make up	concoct

Now try these. Use a dictionary if necessary.

Latin	Prefix	Meaning	English
cresco (cret) I grow	con	grown together, solid	_____
curro (cur, curs) I run	con	go along with	_____
damno (damn) I sentence (in court)	con	find guilty	_____
duco (duc, duct) I lead	con	guide	_____
foedus (fed) alliance	con	friend, ally	_____
fero (fer) I carry	con	talk together	_____
fido (fid, fess)	con	trust in	_____
gredior (gress) I go	con	going together, meeting	_____

CONSTRUCTiON

Try the same with the following words, using the prefix "com".

Latin	Prefix	Meaning	English
bini (bin) two by two	com	put together	_____
memoro (memor) I remind	com	honour by mentioning	_____
mando (mand) I entrust	com	trust with an order	_____
miser pitiable	com	have pity with or for	_____
mitto (mitt) I send	com	give or send with, trust	_____
moveo (mot) I move	com	violent movement, uproar	_____
pono (pos) I place	com	put together	_____
plico (plex) I wind	com	wound together, difficult	_____

Now the same again with these Greek words:

Greek	Prefix	Meaning	English
metron (metr) a measure	sym	of equal measurement	_____
phoneo (phon) I sound	sym	music for a full orchestra	_____
agoge bringing, leading	syn	Jewish meeting place	_____
chronos (chron) time	syn	make watches agree	_____
onyma (onym) name	syn	word which means the same as another	_____
lambano (lab) take	syl	letters taken together to make a sound	_____

Inventaword

These prefixes are excellent ones to play word invention with. In fact, they are so common that you could find that you have invented a word which actually exists!

Here are some of my ideas:

synagorate: to meet in the market place.
convious: the state of a road which has many turn-offs.
sylloutron: a bath big enough for two.
concapellation: spending time with she goats.

Now you try some.

3. GRAMMAR

Exercise 1: Using Latin and Greek

With the knowledge you now have, you should be able to guess at the meaning of some Latin and Greek words.

What do the following Latin words mean?

comparatio
confirmatio
communitas
commotio
concordia

Try the same with these Greek words. Write them out in English letters first:

συμπαθεια
συμμετρος
συνθετος
συμφωνια
συμβολιχος

Revision

You now know the following parts of speech: noun, verb, adjective, adverb, pronoun.

Exercise 2

Refer to the Artemis story and find five examples of each of the parts of speech you know. Quote the line number of each one you find.

Exercise 3

You will find some sentences below which have the name of a part of speech instead of the proper word. Simply replace the name with a word (of that part of speech) which fits well and makes sense.

E.g.: I will **verb** you with an **adjective** stick so **adverb** that your **noun** won't recognise **pronoun**.

This could be: I will **hit** you with a **heavy** stick so **cruelly** that your **mother** won't recognise **you**.

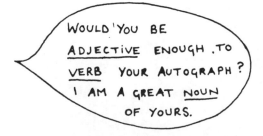

Try that with the following:

    I refuse to mark your **noun** because it is so scruffy. If **pronoun verb** write more **adverb** than this you will have to have **adjective** lessons.

And:

    We would all have been **adverb** destroyed by the **noun** if Superman had not **verb** and taken **pronoun** off to shelter behind a(n) **adjective** rock.

Exercise 4

Here is the description of programmes to be shown on T.V. I have changed some details of it. I have also missed out some words. Put words in which will make sense of the piece, and then name the part of speech for each word you have chosen.

    The Terror Without a Face: a science fiction thriller about three _____ found _____ near an American army base in Canada. A post mortem reveals that the brain and spine have been _____ removed from _____ . But they _____ by night.

Try another:

    The Equalizer: Mama's boy. When McCall, a _____ secret agent, is asked by a desperate _____ to help safeguard her son from the world of drugs, he _____ undercover as an international drug smuggler.

And . . .

    The Muppet Show: Miss Piggy _____ well and _____ upstaged by _____ Ethel Merman, _____ sings a medley of _____ from _____ Broadway composers.

Unit 9: Hermes

1. HERMES

The sun was warm and the air was clear.   Apollo had been
entrusted with the care of the cattle. They seemed content enough
to graze, so the god of music and poetry fell to thinking about
other things. Every now and then he cast a casual eye on the herd
5 to see that all was well. But something felt amiss. Was·the herd
as big as it had been the last time he looked? He counted heads
and noticed that there were some missing. He went to look for
them, and in case there were rustlers about, he put on his cloak
which made him invisible. He soon established that they had not
10 wandered off by themselves. If they had, they would surely have
made for the nearby spring to drink.

Then he came across a cave. "If I were a rustler," he thought, "this would be the place to hide my booty."

He looked around and found plenty of hoof prints in the dust.
15 But they all went away from the cave. There were none to indicate that any had been recently driven into it.

Nevertheless he decided to investigate. He went into the cave through its narrow entrance, which opened up into a large, rocky-roofed cavern. The only light entering the cave came through the
20 narrow opening, so Apollo did not at first see the cot tucked away in the corner. When he did see it he approached carefully and looked in. He saw a baby, clearly only days old, sleeping peacefully. Its little legs were curled up to its body and its thumb was in its mouth, although it was not sucking.

25 Apollo removed his cloak of invisibility and kicked the cot. "All right, Hermes, the game's up," he said.

The baby awoke, saw the god's face, and burst into tears, little fits of crying broken only by sharp intakes of breath.

"You can stop that now and tell me where the cattle are."

30 The crying calmed, and then ceased completely. The baby grabbed the side of its cot and pulled itself up to look at Apollo.

"I'm afraid you'll have to speak to my parents, and they're not around just now. As you can see, I'm a completely helpless day old baby, capable, at the moment, of nothing but sleeping and
35 feeding. Good bye." The baby settled down again to sleep.

"Hermes, do not try it on with me. It's Apollo here, and I know full well about you and your tricks. It was cunning to steal my cattle without my noticing, but dragging them into your cave by their tails! Even I was nearly fooled into thinking that cattle
40 had only left the cave today. Still, it's over. Just tell me where you have hidden them and I'll be off."

"You really don't understand, do you?" Hermes replied. "I can hardly crawl, let alone walk. Look how tender my little feet are." He thrust a little foot into the god's face. "No, all I want is
45 my comfortable cot and my mother's milk to make me into a big strong boy."

Apollo was at a loss what to do. His first inclination was to give the baby a good thumping, but that would not be appreciated by the rest of the gods. As he walked around the cave deep in
50 thought, he heard a tune such as he had never heard before. It was clear, flowing and beautiful. He turned to the cot and saw the baby playing an instrument. There were seven strings stretched

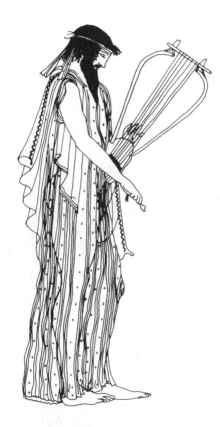

over a turtle shell, and as the baby plucked or strummed, a beautiful sound emerged.

55   Apollo took the instrument from the baby's little hands and tried it himself. It made a wonderful sound that pleased the god of music. He then heard another instrument picking up the tune he was playing. It was that baby again! This time it was blowing into a series of reeds which had been tied together in ascending
60 lengths so that each pipe made a different note. It was difficult not to be captivated by Hermes' cunning and charm.

Pan playing the pipes

    "Who did you steal these from?" he asked. The baby smiled. "I didn't. I made them. Really. You're right about the cattle. I did steal them and dragged them by their tails into the cave.
65 You'll find them tethered round the corner. But these really are mine. The stringed instrument is a lyre. I call it that because it looks like the tail of a lyre bird. The pipes are also my idea."

Apollo was ready to trade. "We could do a deal," he said. "You keep the cattle and I take the instruments."

70   Hermes leaned out of his cot, slapped the palm of Apollo's hand with his, and shouted "Done!"

"Perhaps I have been," thought Apollo.

Hermes had done his first deal on the first day of his life. He grew to be the god of doing deals. He watched over merchants.

75 But as some deals can involve trickery, he was the god of thieves too. He would protect the merchants who were on the road, and also the thieves who preyed on them.

Zeus soon saw that he had a job for a god like this. Someone who knew his way around and was as persuasive as Hermes

80 would make a perfect messenger for Zeus. From then on the god carried a staff to show that he was a messenger, and wore winged sandals to speed him about his work.

Exercise 1

1) Why was Apollo deceived by the tracks of the cattle?
2) Why was he surprised on entering the cave?
3) What was unexpected about the way Hermes replied to Apollo?
4) What deal did the two gods do?

Exercise 2

1) What aspects of daily life led the Greeks to adopt Hermes as a god?
2) Are there any aspects of Hermes' character that you particularly like or dislike?
3) The Roman name for Hermes is Mercury. A rival of British Telecom has taken the name Mercury. Is it a good name for the business? If so, why?
4) Travellers are probably more troubled by thieves and pick pockets than most other people. Why, then, do you think the Greeks could accept Hermes as a god both of travellers and thieves?
5) What jobs in our society would be most likely to attract Hermes?

2. WORDPLAY

Arty and Crafty

There is probably a subject on your timetable called "art". Think of the activities involved in an art lesson.

You may have "art and craft". Do you do the same things as in art?

Then there is "craft design technology". What would you expect to do in these lessons?

Then think of the difference between calling someone "arty" and "crafty".

It looks like the word "art" can be used in many different ways. But if we can find some sense of the word which applies to all the uses of it mentioned above, perhaps we will get to the meaning of the word.

In each case we understand the use of human skill rather than the working of nature. The artist, craftsman and technologist obviously have skills they can use to produce whatever they intend to. A crafty person likewise can use such a situation to his advantage.

The Latin word *ars* means practical skill, learning, or even deceit.

Try to think of three activities an artist might be involved in.

Here's a start: painting, photography . . .

Techne in Greek has a similar meaning.

Think of three things a "technologist" might do for a living. Hermes was arty *and* crafty. He invented musical instruments and could play them beautifully. He could also charm other people to get himself out of trouble. As god of merchants you could say he knew the art of commerce. As god of thieves he had to be pretty crafty.

Muses

The Greeks acknowledged nine goddesses of the arts called the **Muses**. Each one looked over a particular art form:

An artful dodge

Name of the Muse	What the name means	Her art form
Calliope	beautiful voice	recited poetry
Clio	to tell of	history
Erato	= *eros*: love	love poetry (often saucy)
Ourania	= *ouranos*: sky	astronomy
Euterpe	delight well	non religious music
Polyhymnia	of many hymns	religious music
Thaleia	blooming	comedy
Melpomene	singing	tragic poetry
Terpsichore	enjoying the dance	dance

As you can see, the Muses are responsible for all aspects of the arts.

The word *museum* means "a place for the Muses".

How do you think the ancient idea of a *museum* differed from the modern one? You could consider, for instance, whether a dance hall or disco could be called a museum.

The Greek word *mousikos* means "skilled in the things the Muses care for".

If we call someone "musical", what do we mean?

If the Greeks called someone *mousikos*, what would they have meant?

The Name of the Muse

Look at the names of the following Muses:

Calliopē
Euterpē
Polyhymnia
Melpomenē

Each carries a prefix which we see in many English words:

call or **cal, kall** or **kal**	means "beautiful"
eu	means "well"
poly	means "many"
mel	means "song"

Exercise 1

Using a dictionary find as many English words as you can that carry these prefixes and express their meanings. E.g.:

calligraphy = *beautiful* writing
polygon = a figure with *many* angles.

Now look at Polyhymnia and Terpsichorē. See what they are the Muses of. Can you find any English words which look like *hymnia* and *chorē* and are appropriate to these Muses?

Exercise 2

The Muses were the children of Zeus and Mnemosynē. Her name means "memory". The ancients thought more of a person with a good memory than perhaps we do.

Try to think of some arts where it is an advantage to have a good memory. How about starting with an actor?

Also remember, there was a time when the Greeks had no alphabet and could not write as we do. Would memory be more important then?

Exercise 3

If *Euterpe* means "to delight well", and *Terpsichore* means "delighting in the dance", what does *terp* mean?

Can you think of any cartoons to illustrate the meaning of some of the words you have learned?

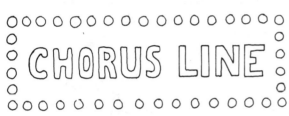

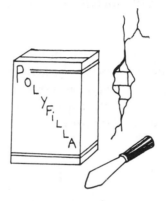

Exercise 4: Inventaword

What is a "musicologist"? Remember that the -logy suffix means "a study of". Using the suffixes -logy, -graphy, invent some subjects for study using the ancient word elements you have seen in this section. E.g.:

polychoreologist: someone who studies many kinds of dances.
Remember to define your new word.

3. GRAMMAR

Exercise 1: Using the Greek Alphabet

Write out the names of the Muses in Greek characters:
Calliopē   Cliō   Eratō   Ourania   Euterpē
Polyhymnia   Thalia   Melpomenē   Terpsichorē

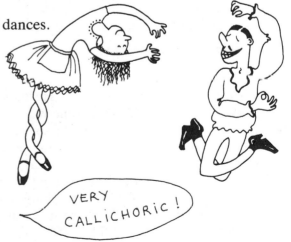

Exercise 2

Below you will find five lists of ancient words. Choose any three words from each list and attempt to define them. You are given some vocabulary to help you. (*multi* (Latin) = πολυ (Greek))

πολυγωνος	*multitudo*	καλλιγραφια	ευαγγελια	μελουργος
πολυμαθης	*multiformis*	καλλιαστραγαλος	ευβουλευς	μελογραφια
πολυμετρος	*multiplico*	καλλιεργια	ευγενεια	μελοποιεω
πολυτεχνος	*multicavus*	καλλιπροσωπος	ευγλωσσια	μελωδια
πολυχρωματος	*multiplex*	καλλισταδιος	ευδικια	
πολυγαμια	*multiplicatio*	καλλιφωνια	ευμαθης	

Vocabulary:

γωνια, angle
μαθη, learning, knowledge
μετρον, a measure
τεχνη, skill
χρωμα (χρωματ-), colour
γαμος, wedding

cavus, hollow
αστραγαλος, ankle
εργον, work
προσωπον, face
σταδιον, stadium

φωνη, voice
αγγελια, news
βουλευς, adviser
γενεα, family
γλωσσα, tongue
δικη, justice

εργον (ουργον), doing
ποιεω, I make
ωδη, song

Exercise 3

Complete the following phrases or sayings:
Lock, stock _____ barrel.
To be _____ not to be.
Rock _____ roll.
Regrets, I have a few, _____ then again, too few to mention.
(Same song) . . . _____ what's a man . . .?
Can you see what job the words you have chosen are doing?

Exercise 4

Here is a section from the story of Hermes. Don't look back to the story. You will notice that some words have been left out of this version. Fill in the gaps to make sense of the passage:
"It's Apollo here, _____ I know full well about you _____ your tricks. It was cunning to steal my cattle without my noticing, _____ dragging them into your cave by their tails! Even I was nearly fooled into thinking that cattle had only left the cave today. Still, it's over. Just tell me where you have hidden them _____ I'll be off."

Polycephalic
What do you think κεφαλη means?

Now compare the words you have inserted with the original version. You might have put in the actual words of the original. You might have some differences. But if your version makes good sense, then you will, at least, have put in the right part of speech.

We are concerned with little words like "and", "but", "or", "for", "either", "now", or "so". Their job is to join together words or phrases, as in "rhythm and blues".

The Latin for "joining" is *junctio*, and "together" is *con*. So a joining together word is called a **conjunction**. You can see that conjunctions are needed to make decent sense of a piece of English, and without them it seems bitty, disconnected or not joined up.

NO "IFS" AND "BUTS" — JUST DO IT!

HARDY CONJUNCTION LAUREL

Here are some more examples of the conjunction: "however", "although", "yet", "if", "unless".

These are not the only ones. To spot a conjunction, just check to see that it is doing a "joining job". You can also check in your dictionary.

Exercise 5

Below is the horoscope page from a magazine. Pick out any ten conjunctions.

SCORPIO OCT 24-NOV 22

Financial problems, which you thought had disappeared earlier this year, are unfortunately back again. But this really is the final sort-out. Get cracking with all joint arrangements before June 21. Thereafter, rising confidence and a lighter tone set you free from all the tangles to do as you wish. In early July you know your life is precisely where you want it to be, and others recognise your influence and standing at last. Affection is offered on the 8th, but beware – the 9th to 11th could cost you dear.

CAPRICORN DEC 24-JAN 20

Underlying problems of a psychological nature are making you tense and edgy around June 20. All you can do is unload as much rubbish as possible from your past, your attitudes and your emotions. By the 21st you are ready to share again with close partners in a meaningful way. Future plans are coming together nicely in July, and one influential friendship has grown enormously. You are now feeling secure and supported, but your tongue is still a little over-sharp. Watch your step around the 9th.

AQUARIUS JAN 21-FEB 18

Having fun today and completely ignoring tomorrow is how you see life at the moment. But decisions must be made around June 20 as future plans will not be put aside any longer. Friends are putting you into a tense, erratic, tetchy state. Hard work follows after the 21st for four weeks. Try a new health regime now as you need to stay fit to keep your head above water. Your career path seems much more settled by early July. Friends, future plans and cash make a very bad combination on the 9th.

PISCES FEB 19-MAR 20

Home is where your heart is, but a heavy workload makes it impossible for you to retreat there too often. June 20 is a fraught day at work but, with Mars in your sign, your battling instincts are up and you will not give in without a struggle. By late June you are in a sunnier mood, happily confident that your firm stand has paid off. An interesting opportunity pops up on July 8. The 9th to 11th is a period of anxiety again but by the 13th the storm has blown over and you are bouncing back with spontaneity and creativity.

TAURUS APRIL 21-MAY 21

Money horrors are back in force around June 20, just as you thought you had them settled for good. Partners seem to be dumping you with more than your fair share of the debt, though your extravagance has been high. In July you appear to have a close partner's full support and colleagues' willing attention to your plans. Now you know how to communicate with influence and clarity, you can begin to breathe a sigh of relief. You will not be able to avoid the cash problems which the 10th brings.

GEMINI MAY 22-JUNE 21

Arguments have you at your wits' end around June 20. An over-critical tongue and a strong need for space have you fleeing the nest and seeking solace in new domains. Mars in Pisces is pushing your ambitions to a cutting edge. You are determined no one will stand in your way. By early July you have work plans and finances firmly under control. Your health has also improved dramatically. Everything is slotting into place now in preparation for the much easier times to come later in the month.

IT'S THE ROCK RADIO CONJUNCTION SHOW. AND HERE'S RANDY BUTTRESS WITH 'IF':
" AND BUT NOW FOR, HOWEVER SO NOR, EITHER ALTHOUGH WHETHER IF OR SO...."

The conjunction is a very common part of speech. At home, try *listening* for them. Listen to a couple of adults speaking, or turn on the radio or T.V.

Listen until you have counted ten conjunctions. Either count them on your fingers or tick them off. Then note how long it took for ten to arise. Work out the number used per minute. E.g. if in 10 minutes you hear 20 conjunctions they are being used at the rate of 2 per minute.

Unit 10: Hephaestus

1. HEPHAESTUS

Hephaestus was the blacksmith god, a son of Zeus and Hera. He is one of the few immortals of whom we hear little but good.

The king and queen of heaven did not always enjoy a harmonious married life. Zeus often fell for the charms of some beautiful woman, and Hera was furious at these infidelities. After one of Zeus's adventures, Hera was so incensed that she went on complaining and scolding till he could endure it no longer, but took his wife, queen of the gods, and strung her up in golden chains and left her hanging by the wrists from the high walls of heaven.

Hephaestus was hurt to see this cruel treatment of his mother, and could not stand by while she suffered such indignity. He took hold of her chains and slowly and steadily pulled her back into heaven and released her. He had saved his mother but defied his father. Nobody defied Zeus and went unpunished, not even his son. Zeus took him and threw him over the walls from which his mother had hung, but this time there were no chains to break the fall.

All day and all night he fell. His senses were dulled as he left
20 the bright light of heaven and tumbled through the blackness of the
night sky. But it was no empty sky, and as his eyes became
adjusted to the darkness, he could pick out strange and threatening
shapes. These were the constellations we see in the clear night
sky. Some are harmless, like the Plough, but Hephaestus' fall
25 took him past constellations which threatened destruction. First
there was Draco, the snake, then the Great Bear and Leo the lion.
Safe from their attack, he then passed Cancer the crab with his
death dealing claws, Hydra with its many snake-like bodies, all
poised to strike the unwary, and last of all, the Great Dog.
30 There was a tremendous crash as he struck the earth. From
that moment on he was a cripple. The terrors of the fall were now
past, but not the anguish of his heart when he realised that he was
despised by his father and ignored by his mother. He had saved
her because he loved her, but she had no love for her crippled son.
35 "If I'm not wanted on Olympus, I shall find another home."
The very thought of Olympus and his rejection caused him pain.
Yet he did find friends on earth. These were neither men nor
gods, but horrendous monsters, huge and hairy with one staring
eye, beings which were feared rather than loved. They were the
40 Cyclopes.
Shunning the airy lightness of Olympus, Hephaestus sought
the opposite, and with the help of the Cyclopes set up a forge
under a mountain. Here at last he was happy and able to develop
his abilities as an artist, inventor, technologist, sculptor and
45 worker in metal. Hephaestus sent the exhaust from the forge
through to the top of the mountain and then out into the air. Thus
such mountains get their name from the Roman version of the god,
Vulcan.
Hephaestus first sought a way to get revenge on his mother for
50 her rejection of him. He set to work on a magnificent golden
throne, the sort that any god would be proud to call his own. But
the throne was not all that it seemed. Full of the cunning of the
avenger, Hephaestus had built in a system of springs, hinges,
latches and devices which would entrap anyone who sat on the
55 throne, and not let them free. He sent this throne to Hera: a
present from her rejected, injured son. May she enjoy it!
Hera surveyed the throne with pride. How right for the queen
of heaven, she thought, though she had no thanks for the child
whose very existence was of no concern to her. She stroked the
60 arms and shining golden back of the throne as she walked slowly

round it. It was as though she were determined to get all the pleasure she could out of its appearance before she assumed her rightful place on this magnificent work of art.

65 She sat with all the royal pride of the queen of heaven, but this soon turned to shame, humiliation and anger when she realised that she could not get up again. She was in great distress and begged the other gods to help her, but none was up to understanding the immortal blacksmith's skill. The gods pleaded with Hephaestus to return to Olympus and free his mother.

70 "She has never earned that title" said Hephaestus.

"But what about the dignity due to the queen of heaven?" they replied.

"What about the indignity I have suffered from her all my life!" Hephaestus answered. It was clear that he would not listen

75 to reason, and so a greater persuader than reason had to be found.

'The Forge of Vulcan'
(Velasquez, Prado, Madrid)

A forge is a hot place, and smiths sweat a lot because of the heat of the fire. Dionysus was an unexpected visitor to the forge, but certainly welcome, especially as he had brought a large quantity of excellent wine with him. Hephaestus drank more wine

80 than he could really take, and yet his thirst was not yet quenched. Once he was thoroughly drunk there was no need for force or persuasion. Dionysus simply steered him back to Olympus and set him to work on freeing Hera.

It had not been a very dignified episode for anyone.

85   Though he was happy to stay in his sooty forge far away from the clear air of Olympus, Hephaestus was as subject as any god to the power of Aphrodite, goddess of beauty and love. Inspired by her he had approached Athene and declared his love. Naturally the virgin goddess rejected him, but then Hephaestus was used to
90 this feeling.

    As it happened, Zeus himself had fallen for Aphrodite, but she, to his amazement and annoyance, would have none of it. Zeus devised a punishment for her which appealed to his sense of humour. He announced her betrothal to Hephaestus the
95 blacksmith. It amused the gods greatly to see this matching of beauty and the beast. Zeus wanted to humiliate Aphrodite by binding her to a god who, if noticed at all, was no more than an object of amusement to the others.

    Imagine how Aphrodite felt. She, the loveliest and most
100 desirable of the immortals condemned to marry Hephaestus and live in his filthy forge, far away from the heavenly Olympus. At first Aphrodite was amused by her new situation. She had never experienced anything like this before. But to settle into happily married life was something she was neither willing nor able to do.

105   The goddess who created desire amongst gods and men is the last to reject any passing fancy, and soon she became attracted to her divine opposite. Love fell for War. Aphrodite and Ares were in love. For some time their affair went unnoticed. Aphrodite used all her skills to conceal the fact.

110 But whatever happens during the day happens under the gaze of Phoebus, god of the sun. He had seen Ares and Aphrodite meet, and had witnessed their wicked behaviour. Outraged by this, he told Hephaestus what was going on.

Hephaestus knew only too well what it felt like to be hurt, but
115 even that did not soften the pain he now felt. But he could strike back. He had an inventive mind and the skills to match. What could technology do for him now?

He hobbled off to the forge and ordered his helpers to fire up the furnace. He had in mind a work such as had never been seen
120 before. It would be a product of the forge, but so fine that it would be scarcely visible. He drew the metal out into strands as fine as those of a spider's web. He bent the strands into loops, and then intermeshed these loops. A net began to form. It was so delicate that if you picked it up you would scarcely feel it. It
125 would simply fall into the shape of your hand. Yet it was so strong that no effort could break it.

When the work was finished the god placed the net around the couch Aphrodite and Ares shared when they met, then told Aphrodite that he would not see her for a while. He was off to
130 visit old friends at Lemnos.

Aphrodite needed no more prompting, but immediately arranged to meet Ares. They thought they were quite safe with Hephaestus away, but then Hephaestus sprung his trap. He had invited the other gods to his house, and when he was sure that
135 Ares and Aphrodite were well caught in the fine meshes of his net, threw open the door and admitted all the immortals to the shameful scene which was being enacted in Hephaestus' own house.

The gods laughed uncontrollably when they saw what
140 Hephaestus had done. "Hephaestus, the slowest of the gods, has overtaken swift Ares by his skill."

Then Apollo spoke to Hermes: "Would you object to being trapped on a couch with Aphrodite?"

"Given the chance, I would be happy to be doubly trapped,
145 and be caught by more witnesses than this, for the chance to lie beside Aphrodite."

Amid the general laughter, Poseidon drew Hephaestus aside and spoke to him: "It is not right to keep these gods tied up like this. You know you have to release them, and I promise that Ares
150 will pay for what he has done."

"But what if he doesn't?" replied Hephaestus. "What if he

tries to slip away and escape his debt altogether?''

"He will not," replied Poseidon. "But even if he does, I promise to pay you whatever has been agreed."

155   And so the lovers were freed, and Hephaestus was satisfied that he had had his revenge.

Exercise 1

1)   How did Hephaestus first offend Zeus?
2)   How was he punished?
3)   How did this punishment affect the rest of his life?
4)   What revenge did he get on Hera?
5)   What state was he in when brought back to free her?
6)   Look at the picture. Identify the things Hephaestus has made.

Hephaestus, then, was the blacksmith god. He tamed the creative fire. This was not the fire of the hearth, but that which can be harnessed in a forge to create great works of technology, art, or everyday use. The Greeks knew how to use metal, and needed great supplies of it properly worked for peaceful or warlike purposes. Thus Hephaestus was a god of considerable importance to them.

Exercise 2

1)   What feelings led Hephaestus to prefer life on earth rather than Olympus?
2)   Try to imagine what Hephaestus would be thinking about as he fell. What were his emotions, and his hopes and fears?
3)   Imagine Hephaestus' forge. Describe how you see it. You could write a poem or draw a picture.
4)   Is there any similarity between the way the gods treated Hephaestus, and the way some people behave towards others?

2. WORDPLAY

Doers

In the story about Hephaestus the god was described in various ways: he was an artist, inventor, worker and so on. These words all have something in common: they all tell us what Hephaestus did. An inventor is a man or woman who invents, a worker works, a sculptor sculpts and so on.

It would be helpful if we could find a part of the word, a prefix or suffix, which would alert us to the fact that we are dealing with someone who **does** something.

From what you have already seen, can you think of some? If you have difficulty, write a list of names for people who **do** something, and look at that list.

We are looking at suffixes again, and the commonest are -er (from Old English) and -or (from Latin).

Exercise 1

Fill in the gap (use a dictionary if you get stuck):

a person who defends is a   _____
             forges   _____
             does   _____
             sails   _____
             thinks   _____
             writes   _____
             directs   _____
             conducts   _____
             advises   _____

Exercise 2

Now try to work out the meaning of the following Latin words:

administrator   *navigator*
debitor   *spectator*
orator   *inventor*
negotiator

We have also learned from the story that Hephaestus was an artist and technologist. The "-ist" suffix also means someone who does something, e.g. cyclist. It can also mean someone who believes in something: capitalist, communist, humanist, etc. Use this -ist suffix, which comes from Greek, in the next exercise.

Exercise 3

Complete the following with an -ist word:
    a _____ looks after your teeth.
    a _____ uses terror to get his way.
    a _____ studies physics.

Funis is the Latin for "rope". *Ambulo* is the Latin for "I walk". What is a "funambulist"?

Somnis is Latin for "sleep". Construct a Latin based word meaning "sleepwalker", using funambulist as your model.

Exercise 4: Believers

The following all indicate someone who has a belief. Fill in the gaps:
    someone who believes in baptism is a _____ .
    someone who believes in royalty is a _____ .
    someone who believes in peace at all costs is a _____ .

There are many other suffixes which indicate a "doer". The following are all from Latin:
    ant: occupant
    arian: librarian
    ate: magistrate
    tor: manipilator

Exercise 5: Inventaword

Using your ancient words list and the new suffixes you have
learned, invent some words to describe someone who does
something. E.g.:

    sacrosagittarian: a holy archer.
    arachnimetrist: someone who measures spiders.

3. GRAMMAR

Using the Greek Alphabet

Look at the following Greek words. Write them out in English
letters. See if you can work out a definition. You are given some
clues.

    αγωνιστης (αγων, a competition)
    κιθαριστης (κιθαρα, a harp)
    φροντιστης (φροντις, a thought)
    οικιστης (οικος, a house)

Now give the meaning of the following Latin words:

defensor	*senator*
gladiator	*accusator*
moderator	*clamator*

Exercise 1

Here is a section from the Hephaestus story. Don't refer back to
it. You will notice that some words have been left out. Try to
guess what they are by making sense of the passage.

    "Hera surveyed the throne _____ pride. How right _____
the queen _____ heaven, she thought, though she had no
thanks _____ the child whose very existence was _____
no concern _____ her. She stroked the arms and golden
back _____ the throne as she walked slowly _____ it.
She sat _____ all the royal pride _____ the queen
_____ heaven, but this soon turned _____ shame,
humiliation and anger when she realized that she could not get
up again."

The exercise itself might be simple. Now try to work out what job those words do in a sentence. If you have difficulty, pick on any one word and try to think what information you get from that word.

You will see that these words, which are called **prepositions**, are followed by a noun or pronoun. The Latin prefix *pre* means "before", so you can see that these words get their force by being "positioned before" another word.

A **preposition** + **noun** often tells you where or how something happened:

I sat <u>under the bridge</u>.
I sat <u>on the chair</u>.
He went <u>before me</u>.

They are often little words like "in", "on", "to", "at", "under", "beside", "behind", etc.

Without prepositions to show the relationship between things, the meaning of language becomes unclear:

"We'll have a shoot out ＿＿＿＿＿ town ＿＿＿＿＿ daybreak."

It's no good having a shoot out if you don't know when or where.

THE CAT SAT UNDER THE MAT?

SO WHEN DO YOU GET THERE?

Exercise 2

Here are some phrases and sayings which you may know. Have some fun with them. Spot the preposition and change it for another to change the meaning of the phrase. E.g.:

"Home, home on the range" . . . "Home, home under the range."

Now try these:

I've got you under my skin.
20,000 Leagues under the Sea.
From rags to riches.
Down the hatch.

From the horse's mouth.
Over the top.
Out of the frying pan into the fire.
Under the sun.
Are you in the telephone directory?
She looks good on horseback.

Think up some examples of your own, change the prepositions,
and challenge your friends to work out the original statement.
E.g.:

I'm gonna rock beneath the clock tonight.

Unit 11: Athene

1. ATHENE

Zeus' first wife was Metis. The name means "cleverness". When Zeus discovered that she was pregnant, he feared that the child might be cleverer than himself, and so be dangerous. Zeus adopted his father's method of dealing with this kind of problem.
5 He ate Metis.

Nine months later, Zeus began to suffer splitting headaches. He felt his skull fit to burst, and just had to find a way to relieve the pressure. He summoned Hephaestus to help. He considered the problem and decided to operate. He reached for his axe,
10 raised it high, and, with all the skill of a blacksmith, split Zeus' skull down the middle. From the parting of the bone sprang a full grown girl dressed ready for war. Across her breast she wore the Aegis, a fringed goat skin which, when she shook it, caused terrible storms and struck terror into men's hearts. The
15 combination of her mother's cleverness and the strength and power of her father made Athene a favourite daughter of Zeus.

Like all gods and goddesses, Athene was proud of her
abilities. She breathed the power of invention into people of skill,
and was an inspiration in war to those who helped her. She was,
20 naturally, highly regarded by the Greeks, and especially the
Athenians, to whose city she gave special protection. But the
daughter of Zeus was quick to anger if any mortal tried to go one
better than her.

Arachne was a poor girl who lived with her father. Her
25 mother had died, but she had taught her daughter the skill of
weaving. Arachne became very practised at this and was soon
famous for the beautiful tapestries she could produce. The girl
had, of course, been inspired by the wisdom and craft of Athene,
and the goddess herself became a proud admirer. But Arachne
30 was foolish and denied that the goddess had anything to do with
her art.

No god would listen to that kind of talk. Athene was
offended, and Arachne made things worse by declaring that she
was prepared to challenge Athene in open competition. She
35 believed her weaving was better than Athene's, and so her skill
was all her own. Athene took action.

There was a tapping at the door of Arachne's cottage. The
girl opened the door to reveal an old woman with straggly white
hair and clothed in pathetic rags. She supported her old bent body
40 on a stick and walked with the slow deliberation of a very old
person. She said that she had heard of the girl's work and had
come to admire it.

Arachne was always happy to receive praise, and proudly
displayed the best of her work.

45 "You're good," said the old woman, "but I would like to give
you a bit of advice." At this, Arachne would raise her eyes to the
sky and smile to herself. She didn't need advice. "You shouldn't
keep saying that you are better than Athene. You know that's not
right, and you are just asking for trouble. I am sure that if you just
50 accepted that she is your inspiration, she would forgive you and
the whole matter would be forgotten."

"You don't understand," said Arachne. "You're not as young
as you were, my dear. Leave me to run my own life. The fact is
that I have challenged Athene, and if she were better than me, she
55 would have the courage to take me on." The old woman changed
her expression. She did not now look like someone giving kindly
advice. The girl felt uncomfortable, but her arrogance kept her

calm. "If you really know so much, tell me why she doesn't come here herself."

60 The old woman straightened up. She stood much taller than Arachne had imagined possible from her appearance. The white left her hair, her features became smooth and glowing, and, as the rags fell from her shoulders, the warlike dress revealed her as Athene. But even then the girl would not give in. Her foolishness 65 had become sheer madness, and she challenged the goddess there and then.

Two looms were set up, one at each end of the room. News soon got out that a competition was on, and people made for the house to watch. The goddess and the girl set to work. They tied 70 their threads to pointed wooden shuttles which were then woven through the vertical threads of the loom. The onlookers fell silent, and the only sound to be heard was that of the shuttle hitting the wooden side of the loom, soon to be returned to beat the other side. Then came the swish of the comb as it pushed the loosely 75 woven threads into a mass towards the top of the loom.

The scenes they were weaving gradually began to appear. Athene depicted herself presenting the olive tree to Athens. It was this gift which led the Athenians to adopt her as their special goddess. They even took their name from her. The other gods 80 were watching, all recognisable because of the perfect detail of the work. All around the central scene were pictures of mortals suffering because they had not acknowledged the superiority of the gods. Here lay a warning for Arachne if she wanted to see it.

Arachne made things worse for herself by depicting the gods 85 taking advantage of innocent young girls. Zeus got his evil way by turning himself into a bull, a swan, a shower of gold, or even a flame. Other gods became horses, birds or even bunches of grapes. Arachne made sure that any god she depicted was acting shamefully.

90 Both works were finished. The purple, gold and silver thread had all been used up, and the looms stood as though proud of the scenes they carried. Athene now approached Arachne's work and inspected it closely. What really upset her was that she could find no fault in it. She could have made the girl look stupid for the odd 95 slipped stitch, but there was none. She was furious. She tore Arachne's work to pieces, ripping it with her nails and throwing the fragments about the room. She then took the heavy wooden shuttle and hit Arachne about the head with it.

At long last Arachne realised she had met her match. There

100 was nothing she could do against a goddess and she had to
recognise the fact. She ran away to her room and shut the door
behind her.

When Athene burst into the room she found Arachne hanging
by a rope which she had tied to a roof beam. At last the goddess
105 felt some pity for the foolish girl, and decided that she should at
least live.

"You can hang from the roof beams if that's what you want,"
said Athene. "But I don't want you dead. You could be a useful
lesson to others." Athene took out a potion which had been
110 prepared for her by Hecate, queen of the witches. As she poured
the liquid over Arachne's head her hair fell out. Her nostrils and
ears receded into her face and her head contracted almost into
nothing. The whole body began to shrink and then absorbed her
arms. Thumbs disappeared, but her fingers, four on each side of
115 her body, were turned into legs. The rest was all belly.

This did not stop Arachne weaving. Her webs were still
perfect, but a web is only a web. She kept her skill but lost her
art.

When you see a spider, remember Arachne, and the power of
120 the gods.

Exercise 1

1) What was unusual about the birth of Athene?
2) How was the goddess dressed at her birth? Why was this?
3) What was the start of the trouble between Arachne and Athene?
4) How did Arachne provoke the goddess in her weaving?
5) How was Arachne punished?

Exercise 2

1) Why did the Greeks make Athene the daughter of Metis?
2) Some of the greatest advances in Greek and Roman science were made by military engineers working on artillery. What might this fact have to do with Athene?
3) If we still believed in Athene as goddess of inventive skills, what projects would she be most interested in now?
4) Is there any justice in the punishment of Arachne?
5) Try to imagine yourself as Arachne changing into a spider. What thoughts would go through your head? What would you have done if you could live through the last few hours again? What things in human life would you miss most as a spider?
6) Find out what it means to be under someone's "aegis". Then try to explain this common phrase.

2. WORDPLAY

Lots of Legs

To a Greek the word *arachnid* would mean "child of Arachne". It still does mean that, in a way. Look the word up to see what it means.

You see that any arachnid is a member of the same family of living things.

There are many ways of putting living things into groups (we call this "classifying"). One of the commonest is by the number of legs they have.

The Latin for "foot" is *pes*, the Greek is *pous*. From these we get the biological suffixes "ped", "pod", "pus", "pede".

So, you are a bi-ped because you have _____ legs.

An octopus gets its name because it has _____ _____ .

BIPED WITH A DEAD LEG

Exercise 1

Define and give an example of each of the following. If in difficulty use a dictionary.

monopod	ocotopod
biped	centipede
tripod	millepede
quadruped	polypod
hexapod	cephalopod (*cephalos* is Greek for head!)

Exercise 2: Terrible Lizards

Greek for a lizard is *sauros*. Biologists refer to the family of reptiles as "sauria".

The Greek word *deinos* means "terrible". So what would you call a "terrible lizard"?

Below you will find a list of Greek words with their meanings. Work out the dinosaur name you get by adding the suffix "saurus". Then say what the animal's name means in English.

brachion	arm
bronte	thunder
ichthys	fish
tyrannos	tyrant
stegos	roof, cover
spina (Latin)	spine
corythos	crested
skolops	stake
apatos	unable to be punished

When you have done this, see if you can match up the names with the drawings on the next page.

Groups

All living things belong to certain families, groups or classes. We have just looked at "dinosaurs". We are "humans", and we have learned about the origin of "spiders".

Biologists divide all living things into such groups. When they do this, they begin with a large group and end up with a small one. For instance, "robins" are a smaller group of the larger group "birds".

Look at the list of Latin and Greek words given below:

Greek		Latin	
chorde	string, anything that joins	*animalia*	animals
		carnis	meat
mamme	breast, teat	*voro*	I eat
-idae	family of	*canis*	dog
tracheia	rough	*lupus*	wolf
phyton	plant	*familiaris*	of the family, domesticated
pteron	wing, feather		

opsis	look, appearance	*primus*	first
strobilos	twisted, like a pine cone (refers to the shape of a cone. Can also mean pirouette)	*homo*	man
		sapiens	thinking, wise
		planta	plant
		coniferalis	cone bearing
		pineus	of the pine
		pinus	pine

All these words are used in biological grouping (or "classification") of living things. Here is a biological classification of the "white pine":

Kingdom (the biggest group):	plantae (plants)
Phylum (Greek = race: the next biggest group	tracheophyta (rough plant)
Class:	pteropsida (looking like a wing or feather: i.e. the leaf)
Order:	coniferales (cone bearing)
Family:	pinaceae (pines in general)
Genus: (Latin = sort, kind):	pinus (the pine tree)
Species (Latin = appearance):	pinus strobus (twisted pine), which we now call the white pine

So when using a biologist's classification system, you start with the biggest group a living thing can be in, and work gradually down until you reach the smallest.

PUNCH   HARD PUNCH   HARD PUNCH ON THE NOSE.

Exercise 3

Look at the two biological definitions below. Using the words you have been given, define each stage (as I have in brackets in the example above), and then try to work out what the animal or plant is.

Kingdom:	animalia	animalia
Phylum:	cordata	cordata
Class:	mammalia	mammalia
Order:	carnivora	primates
Family:	canidae	hominidae
Genus:	canis	homo
Species:	canis lupus	homo sapiens

What animal would it be if Species in the first example read: Canis Familiaris?

It is sometimes necessary to be careful when classifying things. What is wrong with this statement?

"All apples are fruit, therefore all fruit are apples."

This is to do with the fact that bigger groups contain smaller ones.

Inventaword

Using ancient words, invent a new dinosaur and either describe it or draw and label it. Mine is a "spherosaurus".

3. GRAMMAR

As you have seen, one way of classifying animals is by the number of legs they have. Here are the Greek and Latin numbers 1-10.

Latin	Greek	French, Italian, Spanish?
unus	εις	
duo	δυο	
tres	τρεις	
quattuor	τεσσαρες	
quinque	πεντε	
sex	εξ	
septem	επτα	
octo	οκτω	
novem	εννεα	
decem	δεκα	

Exercise 1

Column 3 is there for you to fill in any numbers you might know in any of these languages. You may have picked them up on holiday.

See how closely the numbers in these languages correspond.

Then write down as many words you can think of which derive from Latin or Greek numerals, e.g. unit, union; duo, duet, duel etc.

It should be clear that these Latin and Greek words supply our language with many related words.

Have you written September, October, November, December? If so, why should they be the 9th, 10th, 11th and 12th months? The answer is that the Roman year ran from March to February. Now check your 7th, 8th, 9th and 10th months.

You now know the English parts of speech. The language also has a form or structure. This is a bit like a skeleton, because without its structure you would be unable to recognise parts of the language and therefore unable to make sense of it.

A **verb** is a **doing word**. Sentences generally need verbs. If you doubt it, try writing one without a verb. There will usually be someone or something to do the verb. And this will be the **subject**

of the sentence. There will often be someone or something acted on by the verb. This will be the **object of the sentence**.

Subject	Verb	Object
Flash Gordon	saves	the Universe
I	like	the Universe
I	thank	Flash Gordon

Notice too how the order of words in English is so important: "Flash Gordon beat the Martians" is quite different from "The Martians beat Flash Gordon".

SORRY FLASH!

In one Flash Gordon is the subject, in the other he is the object. In the one, Martians are the object, while in the other, they are the subject.

Exercise 2

Pick out five sentences from the story of Athene. Write them out and mark the **subject, verb** and **object** of each sentence.

Exercise 3

Here is a short passage. In two cases the subject and object of the
sentence have been changed round. Try to find them, and rewrite
the passage so that it makes sense.

"It was maths and it was hard. The problem had to solve the
boy before he could go home. Nor did he want to be late. A
special dinner had prepared mother, and she would be upset if
he weren't there."

And again:

"The monkeys were feeding the zoo keepers. It was always an
amusing scene. The bananas were allowed to offer spectators
to the monkeys. How delicious!"

Now write a passage yourself with some subjects and objects
reversed. Challenge your friends to correct it.

Unit 12: Ares

1. ARES

The Trojan prince Paris has abducted Helen, the wife of a Greek
king. Determined to bring Helen back to Greece, the Greeks have
been besieging the city of Troy for ten years. The Greek hero
Diomedes, inspired by Athene, is having a particularly good day.

5   The battle at the walls of Troy had taken a brutal turn.
Slaughter was in the air and the blood of the dead and dying had
stained the dry dusty earth black. Lust for blood was in the heart
of the Greek hero Diomedes. He could make no mistakes that
day. Whenever he threw a spear, a man fell. When he lunged
10 with his sword he left a man wounded or dead.

    Ten years the war had been going on, but few could remember
a battle as vicious as this. The gods, too, joined in the fight, and
Aphrodite, goddess of love and beauty, was in the lines of her
beloved Trojans. When she saw their suffering she decided to
15 face Diomedes herself. But not even the goddess could escape his
spearthrust, and, wounded in the hand, she departed.
    She left the battlefield distraught, and asked her brother
Apollo for help. He had often fired his deadly arrows at the

Greek lines, but this time he saw that things had gone too far. He
20 approached the god of war.

"Ares," he said, "we need your help. Diomedes is wild. It's
one thing to kill mortals, but he has wounded Aphrodite. He's so
sure of himself that he's ready to take on Zeus himself."

Ares smiled. He lived for war and loved to be at the head of a
25 battle line. So he got ready to fight.

He protected his legs with bronze greaves, tied a bronze breast
plate to his body and put a tight-fitting helmet on his head. The
tall red plume struck fear into the enemy. He placed a short-
bladed sword in his belt, two long spears in his chariot, and finally
30 took up his shield. It was shaped like a figure of eight, and was
made of layers of ox-hide. He mounted his chariot and called on
his immortal assistants, Enyo, the destroyer of cities, Deimos, the
demon of terror, and Phobos, who inspires panic, to join him.

He then threw a cover of darkness over the battlefield, and,
35 without being seen, joined the Trojan lines. He pulled up close
behind their leader, Prince Hector, who was quick to take
advantage of the cover of darkness and made straight for the
Greeks. Ares followed, and put courage into the hearts of the
Trojans as they met the Greeks face to face. The god hacked his
way through, getting nearer and nearer the Greek quarters and
leaving a trail of corpses behind him. When the Greeks saw what
was happening, their confidence was shaken.

Diomedes quickly realised that Ares had joined the Trojans.
There was no other explanation for this change of fortune. He felt
45 the presence of the god who puts men's lives in the balance. The
last thing his troops must do is panic, because if they scattered,
the Greek camp would be at the mercy of the Trojans. He
ordered his men to fall back and regroup, giving them time to
prepare for the new onslaught.

50 The Trojans struck the Greek line with force. More hand to
hand fighting followed, and as the Greeks fell back, Phobos put
fear into their hearts. The Trojans could smell success. In no
time, Hector and Ares were pushing ahead, trampling over the
bodies of the men they had killed, and the river Scamander, where
55 the women of Troy had, in times of peace, washed clothes, now
ran red.

Hera loved the Greeks, and she was troubled to see their line
falling back and the hero Diomedes struck by an arrow. She went
to Athene and said, "This is a disaster. Ares will slaughter
60 anyone who gets in his way. Battles are to be lost or won, but

there is no need for a bloodbath like this. But Ares has tasted blood and he will carry on until he has had his fill. He must be stopped.

The two goddesses approached Zeus. "Look how Ares is
65 behaving on the battlefield. This is butchery, not war. He won't stop until there are no Greeks left to kill. Will you be angry if we take him on?"

Zeus knew Ares only too well. "Go and deal with him. You, Athene, know about tactics in battle. You can't take him on in a
70 contest of strength, so go and outwit him. He might then see that there is more to winning a battle than wiping out the enemy."

Two chariots, each bearing a fully armed goddess, sped down from Olympus and came to a halt where the rivers Simois and Scamander meet. Hera hid the chariots in a cloud and took on the
75 appearance of the Greek hero Stentor. She joined the battle and rallied the troops. "You cannot fall back any more. If you do, the Trojans will be at your camp and destroy the ships which brought you here. You must regroup and take the battle back to the enemy."

80 Meanwhile, Athene went over to Diomedes. He had been hit by an arrow and was cutting the barbed head out of the wound. "You must go back to the fight," she told him.

Diomedes continued cutting around the arrow's head. "Why?" he said. "I know that Ares has joined Hector and no
85 mortal can take him on. The battle is as good as lost. It's only a matter of time."

Athene smiled, got aboard Diomedes' chariot and beckoned him to join her. "I shall be with you throughout the battle."

Diomedes knew that he was in the presence of a goddess and
90 that the odds in the battle were now fairer. He leapt into the chariot and Athene drove into the thick of the fight.

Ares had killed Periphas, a gigantic warrior, and was busy stripping the valuable armour from his corpse. As the chariot approached, Athene made herself invisible. Ares left the body,
95 picked up his spear and waited for the attack. The god skilled in slaughter, known as the butcher, was now pitted against a goddess who understood the tactics of war and ways to win. Athene knew Ares would seek to sidestep the chariot and, with an upward thrust, heave Diomedes out of the vehicle, impaled on his broad
100 bronze spear point.

Diomedes approached.   Ares lunged forward.   Athene

watched, and then brushed away the spear point like a mother
brushing a fly from a sleeping child.

Now Ares' front was unguarded. Diomedes reacted quickly
105 and thrust his spear. Athene grabbed the shaft and directed it at
the god's belly. The bronze point slipped under the breastplate
and opened up a wound which Diomedes enlarged with a vicious
twist of the spear as he withdrew.

Ares stood still for a moment as though he did not know what
110 had happened. He looked at the great gaping wound, held the
edges together, threw back his head and let out a terrible yell.
There was a moment of silence on the battlefield. Ares clothed
himself in a dark cloud and retreated to Olympus like a tornado.

Still clutching his wound he went to Zeus. "See what happens
115 when gods fight! You should never have allowed Athene to take
part in the battle. I had things under control, and now she has
upset everything and I am wounded."

Zeus leaned forward on his throne and frowned at Ares. "It is
only because Hera is your mother that I don't send you down to
120 Hades with the Titans. You revel in slaughter and death, and that
is why you are the most hated of gods. Now don't come to me
and complain that you have been treated the way you like to treat
others."

Ares was dismissed.   He went away and spread divine
125 ointment on his wound which soon healed without a scar. He had
a bath and changed his bloodstained clothes, and, more humbly
this time, took his seat beside Zeus.

Hera and Athene had, for the moment, put a stop to Ares'
butchery.

Exercise 1

1)   What were the two sides in the war which was being fought?
2)   What event led to Ares being asked to take a part in the war?
3)   How did Ares add to the confusion of the battle and so aid
the Trojans?
4)   Which of his helpers did Ares take into battle?
5)   Which goddesses tried to counter the action of Ares?
6)   How was Diomedes' blow at Ares made so effective?
7)   Was Zeus sympathatic to Ares' complaints? How did he
reply to the war god?

Facing Phobos

Exercise 2

1) Why was such an unattractive god as Ares so important to the Greeks?

2) What does the character of Ares tell you about the nature of ancient warfare?

3) What details about heroic warfare do you learn from the passage above? What could Deimos, Phobos and Enyo do in ancient warfare? Could they do anything in modern war? Try to think of actual situations in which you could say they appear.

4) What advantages do you learn gods have over mortals in ancient warfare?

2. WORDPLAY

Horror!

Phobos or "panic" attended Ares in war. How is panic created or used in war?

WARPAINT.

THE APPEARANCE OF WEAPONS.

YOU CANNOT WIN THROW DOWN YOUR ARMS... YOU ARE SURROUNDED...

PROPAGANDA.

AiEEEEEE! GRRRRR

WAR CRY.

There are fears which people have which are irrational or difficult to explain. These are called "phobias" – you can see the connection with Phobos. You have probably heard about "claustrophobia", which means fear of being shut in and it can cause panic. It comes from the Latin *claustra* (lock) and the Greek suffix *phobia*.

Exercise 1

What would "arachnophobia" be? Remember one of the stories you have read. What would an "arachnologist" do?

If a "hydro-electric" system is one which gets electrical power from water, what is "hydrophobia"? (This is a symptom shown by people who have been bitten by an animal carrying "rabies". *Rabies* is the Latin word for "madness".)

Agora is the Greek word for an open space suitable for a market place. What is "agoraphobia"?

Xenos is a Greek word for a person who is a stranger or alien. What is "xenophobia?"

Exercise 2

Try to work about what these forms of xenophobia are:
   Anglophobia
   Russophobia
   Francophobia
   Italophobia

The adjective form of phobia is "phobic". Someone who is afraid of being shut in could be described as "claustrophobic".

   Can you also make another noun from claustrophobic? Someone who is afraid of being shut in is a claustrophobe. What do you call a person who hates the English? He is an _____ .

Exercise 3

Using your ancient words list or a dictionary, define the following:
   Triskaidekaphobe
   Photophobic

Exercise 3: Lovers

The opposite of a phobia is a "philia". That is a Greek word which means "love". So someone who likes the English is an "anglophile". They enjoy "anglophilia".

Give a name to someone who loves things French

> Russian
>
> Italian
>
> foreign

Biblion is the Greek for a book. What do you call someone who loves books?

> *Theke* is the Greek for a case or a chest. What does the French word *bibliotheque* mean? What is a *discotheque*?

Exercise 4

An alternative to the -philia ending is "-phily". The meanings are the same.

Using your ancient words list, define the following:

toxophily	hydrophily
haemophilia	dendrophily

Sometimes the "phil" part comes first in the word, but it still has the same force. As in the last exercise, define the following:

Philip	philomath
philology	Philadelphia
philharmonic	philogyny
philanthropy	philosopher
philhellenic	

Crazies

Mania is the Greek word for "madness". Mania is a word which suggests an unreasonable attraction to something.

For instance, *ego* is both Greek and Latin for "I". You could call someone who is completely self-centred an "egomaniac".

Where a "bibliophile" loves books, someone with "bibliomania" will stop at nothing to get hold of them.

Exercise 5

Again with your list, define the following:

dipsomania   stadiomania
megalomania   hippomania
pyromania   cynomania
Anglomania   tulipomania

Exercise 6

Using phobia, mania and philia invent some words of your own using your ancient words list. Define them, and challenge others to do so. E.g.:

delphinophilia   love of dolphins
grammatistophobe   someone who is afraid of teachers
stadiomaniac   someone who is crazy about horse racing

3. GRAMMAR

Exercise 1: Using the Greek Alphabet

Write out the following in English and say who they are:

αρης   φοβος   ερις   εννω

Write out the following in Greek letters, and say who or what they are:

Diomedēs   Athēnē   Hēra   Aphroditē   Stentōr
Ichōr

You are aware that an **adjective** is a word which describes a person, place or thing. In the story you have heard of "**dry, dusty earth**", "He had often fired his **deadly** arrows", "called on his **immortal** assistants" and so on.

You are also aware that an **adverb** is a word which describes a verb, adjective or another adverb. In the story we have met: "Ares lunged **forward**", "Ares stood **still**", "more **humbly** this time", "Diomedes reacted **quickly**", and so on.

But you can use more than just one word to do the job of an adjective or an adverb. Take the sentence "he fired his **deadly** arrows"
   You could equally say:
   "He fired arrows **which killed**"
   "He fired arrows **with their death dealing barb**"
   "He fired arrows **which found their target and killed their man**"
It simply depends on how the writer wishes to speak to you.

Look at the next group of sentences, and write down the one you like best:
   That is mild mannered Clark Kent.
   That is Clark Kent, who has mild manners.
   That is Clark Kent, a man of mild mannered nature.

Now do the same with these:
   As the sword-wielding devil approached, Indiana Jones turned to his friend and spoke quietly.
   . . . Indiana Jones turned to his friend and spoke in a hushed voice.
   . . . Indiana Jones turned to his friend and spoke in a voice only she could hear.

Again, which one do you like best? Why does the version you have chosen appeal to you?

Exercise 2

Here are two sentences from the story of Ares:

Diomedes is wild.

Diomedes had quickly realised that Ares had joined the Trojans.

Rewrite these sentences, expressing "wild" and "quickly" in more than one word.

Then do the same with:

The battle had taken a **brutal** turn.

Ares stood **still**.

Expressions which do the job of an adjective or an adverb are called **phrases** and **clauses**. It is easy to tell which is a phrase and which is a clause. A clause has a verb in it, a phrase does not. So:

"arrows **with their death dealing barb**" is a phrase.

"arrows **which killed**" is a clause.

Exercise 3

Here are some examples from the story. Write C against a clause, and P against a phrase.

He placed a short bladed sword **in his belt**.

They came to a halt **where the rivers Simois and Scamander meet**.

He protected his legs **with bronze greaves**.

They will destroy the ships **which brought you here**.

Exercise 4

Here are some more sentences. Some contain an adjective, some an adverb. These are printed in bold type. Simply turn the adjective/adverb into either a phrase or a clause. E.g.:

I like the **Lone** Ranger: I like the Ranger who doesn't have a friend.

The Empire strikes **back**: the Empire strikes in return for damage done.

Now try four of these:

. . . where there seldom is heard a **discouraging** word . . .

And the sky is not **cloudy** all day

Here comes Ming the **merciless**

The **Beach** Boys

Enter the classroom **quietly**

Rome, the **eternal** city

Please dispose of litter **thoughtfully**

Blow the wind **southerly**

Bad day at Black Rock

Desperately seeking Susan

Unit 13: Aphrodite

1. APHRODITE

Aphrodite was the goddess of love and beauty. She may have
been soft and sensual, but her power was no less complete than
that of the brutal Ares or wise Athene. Her powers are the
subtlest. You may be trapped and not know it until you meet the
5 object of your love. And when she has sprung the trap on you,
you might as well try to tear your way out of Hephaestus' net.

Eros asleep

Her son, Eros, carried a quiver full of arrows. The arrows
were tipped with a poison, so that if Aphrodite asked Eros to
strike someone, her power got into their blood, and became a part
10 of that person. Nor was it easy to escape Eros' arrows. He was a
deadly shot, and he had wings to speed him wherever his mother
ordered.

One day, while Eros was cradled in his mother's arms, he
made a sudden turn and accidentally grazed her with an arrow.
15 She pushed her son away in pain to examine the scratch. Her
appearance was perfection, and she hated the thought of even the
tiniest mark on her pure skin. But although she had only been
grazed, the poison had entered her, and she didn't know it.

There happened to be a young man out hunting in the wood.
20 He was Adonis. He was handsome, and his physique as perfect
as a mortal's could be. Aphrodite immediately fell in love with
him. Because of the accident with Eros' arrow, she was now
subject to her own power.

No man could resist the advances of the goddess of love, and
25 they spent many long hours happy in each other's company. They
were inseparable, and Aphrodite stayed with him even when he
was hunting. When she realised the danger involved in this sport,
she lovingly gave him this advice: "Don't hunt any animals which
fight back. Chase hare, deer and stags, but steer clear of wild
30 boar, wolves, bears with great claws or lions filled with the flesh of
other beasts. I can't help you against animals which strike back."

Aphrodite had to leave Adonis for a while. She harnessed the
swans which drew her chariot, took the reins and sped off through
the air with a worried backward glance at her love.

35 But Adonis, though warned by Aphrodite, soon became
careless and let his bravery get the better of him. While out
hunting his hounds picked up the scent of a boar. They tracked it
down, and roused it from its lair deep in the wood. The boar,
terrified and dangerous, shot out of the thicket at a charge. It was
40 making for Adonis. He took his stand in the path of the charging
boar. He raised his spear above his head. The balance was
perfect and he could feel the weight of the broad iron head giving a
pleasing spring to the shaft. The boar continued its charge.

Adonis stood his ground.´ He waited as the boar drew nearer.
45 Now it was in range, but he could still miss. Closer came the
boar, but Adonis waited until he knew his aim would be sure.

There were only yards between them when he lunged with the
spear. He was accurate, but not enough so. The point hit the
hard rounded shoulder of the animal and cut it deeply, but the
50 weapon did not lodge tight in the joint. In pain and rage the boar
twisted and writhed and managed to dislodge the spear with its
snout.

Now disarmed and panic-stricken, Adonis ran in search of
some safe place. But the boar was quicker. With a broad
55 sideways sweep, the tusk which curved up and out from the
beast's jaw caught Adonis. The unprotected skin of his belly was
laid open. The boar stopped in its tracks, considering a further
attack. Realising that this was unnecessary it returned to its lair
to lick its wound. Adonis poured out his life-blood on the yellow
60 sand.

As soon as she heard him cry, Aphrodite knew that Adonis
was in trouble. She swung the chariot round and made for the
spot where he lay. She saw his body from a distance. His limbs,
all covered with blood, lay still in the sand. She came to rest
65 beside him, dismounted, and cradled the mangled body in her
arms.

She knew he was dead. She let out a great cry, tore her hair
by the roots and beat her breast with clenched fists, cursing Fate
for letting the boy go. But´there was still something she could do.
70 Although she could not return his body to life, she could make
sure that death was not the end of Adonis.

"Every generation shall remember your death," she cried.
"Every year there will be, as a memorial to my grief, a
reenactment of your death, and the cries of mourning shall be
75 heard all over the earth. I shall make your blood a flower. The
gods have granted this honour to others, so they shall to you."

She took out a phial of nectar, the holy drink of the gods, and
sprinkled it on Adonis' blood. As the liquids mixed, the blood
began to bubble up, and within an hour a delicate plant had
80 formed. Soon a flower had developed, red like the blood of
Adonis. It was beautiful beyond other flowers, as Adonis was
beyond other men. But just as his beauty was short-lived, broken
by a violent blow, so, at the lightest stirring of the breeze, the
petals fell away, and, deprived of its loveliness, the flower died.´

85   The flower is called **anemone,** after the Greek for the wind,
anemos.

Aphrodite was a goddess of immense importance to the
Greeks. She inspired men and gods with love, passion and desire.
These are emotions which can provoke acts of great beauty, but
90 also of great ugliness. If love is returned, the lovers are happy. If
it is not, then hate can quickly grow. People have fought and
killed for love. It would be too easy to think of love as a harmless
feeling. You can be made a slave by it as surely as you could by
your worst enemy.

95   All who are capable of feeling these great emotions are, the
Greeks would say, subject to the power of Aphrodite. She is
appropriate to the life of us all.

Exercise 1

1)   How might you fall under Aphrodite's power?
2)   Who acted as her agent in this?
3)   How did the goddess come to fall for Adonis?
4)   What warning did she give the young man?
5)   What was his fate?
6)   Why should a flower remind you of Adonis?

Exercise 2

1)   What would happen to a people who had no place in their lives for Aphrodite?

2)   The ancients believed that a war could be caused by love. Try to imagine a sequence of events starting with love and ending in war.

3)   All would have been well if Adonis had followed Aphrodite's advice. Why didn't he? Are there any times you have suffered from ignoring advice given you?

4)   Do you know any stories about people who have died for love?

2. WORDPLAY

What's in a Name?

If you call a dog "Fido" you are suggesting that it is faithful, because the name comes from the Latin word *fidelis*, faithful or trustworthy.

Amanda is the Latin for "loveable", while *Peter* means "rock". See if your name is in the list of personal names. It might not be from Latin or Greek. *Adonis* is from Hebrew, the language of the Old Testment of the Bible. The Hebrew word *Adonai* means "Lord".

Now let us see what the names of the Greek gods mean. It is not always possible to work out the meaning of the god's name.

Zeus: Ancient Indian (Sanskrit) *dyauh pitar* = sky father. In Greek it is *Zeu pater*, in Latin *Jupiter*.

Hera: may be related to Greek *hora* = season. Perhaps meaning "ripe for marriage".

Demeter: Greek *mēter* = mother. The *de* is either "earth" or "corn".

Apollo: the Greeks thought it might be from *Apollumi* = I destroy.

Artemis: not known.

Hermes: Greek *herma* is a pile of stones marking the boundary of land. Boundaries are crossed (the travelling messenger) or cheated on (the trickster).

Hephaestus: possibly from the Greek *hapto* = I fasten to, and *aitho* = light up, kindle.

Athene: protectress of Athens.

Ares: an ancient Greek word meaning "the crowd of war".

Aphrodite: *Aphros* = foam. Aphrodite was born from the sea.

Poseidon: Greek *potei* meaning Lord. The rest of the name is difficult. He is the god of the sea. The Romans called him Neptune. He caused earthquakes.

Dionysus: Greek *Dio*, a form of the Greek for Zeus. The rest is uncertain. The Greeks thought it meant "twice born" (remember the Semele story). Some connect it with Mt. Nysa, his supposed birthplace.

When the Greeks mentioned these gods, they often added a word or phrase to describe them. It's like saying "Flash Gordon, **Saviour of the Universe**". Such a word or phrase is called an **epithet** (Greek, meaning "put on").

Exercise 1

You will find below 13 groups of **epithets**. Each group refers to one of the gods.

From what you know of the gods, match each group to one of the gods. The groups are numbered, so all you need write is, e.g., Zeus = no. 9.

The epithets are Greek unless stated otherwise.

1) *kelainephes* (black with clouds)
   brontaios (Gk) *tonans* (Lat)
      (thundering)
   xenios (hospitable)
2) *polias* (protectress of the city)
   polyboulos (wise)
   glaukopis (grey-eyed)
   obrimopatre (daughter of a great
      father)
3) *Zeus katachthonios* (Zeus beneath the
      earth)
   pylartes (gatekeeper)
   Ploutos (Gk) *Dis* (Lat) (wealth)
4) *chalaipous* (trailing a foot)
   mulciber (Lat) (smelter)
   klytotechnes (famous skill)
5) *bromius* (Lat) (revelry, party-going)
   lyaios (loosener up)
   polygethes (giver of joy)
6) *verticordia* (Lat) (one who turns
      hearts)
   philommeidis (lover of laughter)
   machanitis (contriver of things)

7) *aglaokarpos* (bearing good fruit)
   kalliplokamos (with lovely hair)
   bona dea (Lat) (good goddess)
8) *caducifer* (Lat) (wand bearer)
   psychopompos (conducts the dead)
9) *Pythios* (of Pythia. Remember Python)
   hekaergos (far shooting)
   mantis (teller of oracles)
10) *elaphebola* (deer shooting)
    eileithyia (presiding over childbirth)
    potnia theron (mistress of the animals)
11) *gamelia* (presiding over marriage)
    matrona Romana (Lat) (Roman
       mother)
    pronuba (Lat) (prepares the bride)
    boōpis (cow-eyed)
12) *ennosigaios* (earthshaker)
    gaieochos (encircles the earth)
    rector pelagi (ruler of the sea)
13) *enyalios* (warlike)
    ultor (Lat) (avenger)
    gradivus (Lat) (one who marches on)
    alloprosallos (unreliable friend)

Exercise 2: Inventaword

Now, using the words, or parts of them, that you have above, or your ancient words list, produce some epithets yourself. They can be as long and complicated as you wish, and they can describe anyone or anything. Say who or what they describe. E.g.:

   mesoloutrarchos: the leader of the middle of the bath; the god
     of swimming pool attendants.

NOW WELCOME YOUR QUIZMASTER, THE FAR FIRER OF QUESTIONS, THE MAN WITH THE GOLDEN MICROPHONE, THE KEEN-BRAINED SWEET TALKER, LOVER OF LAUGHTER WITH BEAUTIFUL HAIR, THE RIB TICKLER, TELLER OF ORACLES, YOUR VERY VERY OWN.....

'TINKER' TAYLOR !

3. GRAMMAR

Exercise 1: Using the Greek Alphabet

Put the following into Greek letters:

polyboulos   katachthonios   klytotechnēs   psychopompos
gaiēochos

Now you know what a clause and a phrase is, we should think about what they do in a sentence. Look at this verse:

The elephant is a bonny bird,

   It flies **from bough to bough**.

   It builds its nest **in a rhubarb tree**

   And whistles **like a cow**.

The phrases have been printed in bold type. But what job do they do?

   The first two tell us **where** something is happening. The third tells us **how** something is done.

Exercise 2

Now look at the following poem by Edward Lear:
    They went **to sea in a sieve**, they did,
    In a sieve they went **to sea**:
    In spite of all their friends could say,
    On a winter's morn, on a stormy day,
    In a sieve they went **to sea**.

Pick out any two (different) phrases, and say what job they do in
the sentence.

Here's another bit of the same poem. In this you will see phrases
and a clause.
    All night long they sailed away;
    And **when the sun went down**,
    They whistled and warbled a moony song
    To the echoing sound of a coppry gong,
    In the shade of the mountains brown.

The clause is in line two. What job does it do? It tells us **when**
they whistled and warbled. It tells us **the time** when they did the
whistling and warbling.

Now you say what job the phrases do.

Exercise 3

Here is the rest of that verse. The clauses and phrases are in bold
type again. You choose one clause and one phrase, and then say
what job it is doing.
    "O Timballo! How happy we are,
    When we live in a sieve and a crockery jar,
    And **all night long in the moonlight pale**,
    We sail away **with a pea-green sail**,
    In the shade of the mountains brown!"
    Far and few, far and few,
    Are the lands **where the Jumblies live**;
    Their heads are green, and their hands are blue,
    And they went **to sea in a sieve**.

Now let us look back at the story. Here are some sentences with a phrase or clause in bold type. You say whether it is a phrase or a clause, and then what job it is doing in the sentence. It might tell us when or where something is happening, why or how. E.g.:

When she has sprung the trap on you, you might as well try to tear your way out of Hephaestus' net.

This is a clause because there is a verb in it. It tells you something about **the time** of the action.

Try four of these for yourself:

If Aphrodite asked Eros to strike someone, her power got **into their blood**.

He had wings to speed him **wherever his mother ordered**.

One day, **while Eros was cradled in his mother's arms**, he made a sudden turn.

He accidentally grazed her **with an arrow**.

She hated the thought of the tiniest mark **on her pure skin**.

Although she had only been grazed, the poison entered her.

There happened to be a young man hunting **out in the wood**.

His physique was as perfect **as a mortal's could be**.

They spent many long hours happy **in each other's company**.

Aphrodite stayed with him **even while he was hunting**.

When she realised the danger, she gave him this advice.

Aphrodite had to leave Adonis **for a while**.

She sped off **through the air**.

Adonis waited **until he knew his aim would be sure**.

As soon as she heard the story, Aphrodite knew that Adonis was in trouble.

It returned to its lair **to lick its wounds**.

Unit 14: Poseidon

1. POSEIDON

The first inhabitants of the earth lived in the Golden Age, as the
Greeks called it. The people were neither dishonest nor greedy.
The year had no seasons and the earth produced all they needed
to live on, so that the human race did not have to spend its time
5 working. There was no crime, no law, no war, no cities, no ships.

When the Golden Age gave way to the Silver, the seasons
were created, and mortals had to work the land in order to survive.

In the following Age of Bronze they fought each other using
their fists, nails and teeth. They learned to use sticks and stones
10 as weapons, and made axes and spears.

The Age of Iron which followed was the worst the earth had
seen. It was a time of mindless violence. People ripped metals
from the earth to make swords and spears. Rulers emerged who
surrounded cities with defensive walls, and ships put to sea in
15 search of wealth. People lost respect for themselves and others:
families were in conflict, father against son, and brother against
brother. They even lost respect for the gods. The Olympians
looked down on this with displeasure, but their anger turned to
fury when the tyrant Lycaon, a brute who had sunk so low that he
20 had tasted human flesh, announced that Zeus was no god, and
tried to kill him.

Zeus called a council of the gods to discuss the situation. The
earth had once been clean, pure and perfect, but was now stained
by the evil of the human race. The wickedness of the people was
25 an offence to the gods and the rest of nature. Sadly the gods
agreed: destruction was the only action they could take to cleanse
the earth of its wickedness.

Zeus took the thunderbolt in his right hand. The burning
white heat was reflected in his eyes as he raised it high. He drew
30 back his huge right arm and tilted the point towards its target,
gathering all the force of his body behind the throw. Then
suddenly he checked himself. He brought down his arm and
furrows of deep concern appeared on his forehead.

"This bolt will certainly destroy the earth," he said, "but what
35 if its heat proves so great that the air above the earth catches fire?
Before we know it, the blaze could spread all over heaven."

He laid the bolt down because he feared that, in destroying the
human race, he might destroy the whole universe. So he sent the
rain and it fell in torrents for many days and nights till there was
40 no dry place on the earth. But even so, Zeus was not satisfied. It
was at this moment that he called for his brother Poseidon the
Earthshaker, god of the earthquake, god of horses, and god of all
the waters on the face of the earth, both salt and fresh.

Poseidon summoned all the rivers to his palace beneath the
45 sea. There had never been such a gathering before, and each river
eyed his brothers, wondering what Poseidon had in store for them.

"Use your strength as you have never done before," he
ordered. "Flow fuller than you do in spring when the mountain
snow has melted and doubled your power. The rain has already
50 added to your might. Let nothing stand in your way. You have
always been the bringers of refreshment and life. Now be the
bringers of death. Break your banks. Run with such strength that
nothing can stand in your path. The earth will be at your mercy
so long as you wish."

55 The rivers returned to their sources and built up their strength
for the assault. They gathered the water of the snowy mountain
tops, the water of the sky, and all that drained into them through
the sodden earth.

Imagine a team of horses drawing a chariot at the races. They
60 trot, canter, then all gallop together, and, gathering momentum,
they build up to a speed they have never reached before. But they
go so fast that they get out of control. They do not respond to the
charioteer as he struggles to keep them to the right track. If they
tried to turn at that speed, they would fall because they are going
65 so fast. They fail to take a bend and leave the course. So the
rivers gathered momentum until they could not keep within their
banks. All over the earth, rivers left their courses and flooded
over ground where they had never been before. Crops and
orchards, men and animals were swept away.

70   Poseidon himself then raised the trident he always carried,
and, concentrating all the power of the seas behind it, dashed it
against the surface of the earth. All over the earth deep gaping
chasms appeared, and from them a fresh flow of water gushed.
The buildings which were not flattened by the flow were
75 submerged by it.

    After a few days you could not distinguish land and sea. The
whole earth was one great sea, with no shores. Some tried to save
themselves by climbing to the top of tall buildings, or making for
the summits of mountains. Others launched boats because they
80 wanted to save their families, while elsewhere you could see
young sons and daughters left to fend for themselves, or aged
fathers and mothers, tired and deserted, and waiting for death.

    Fish were entangled in the topmost branches of trees, and
there were seals where the goats used to pasture. Dolphins were
85 now the lords of the woodlands, while wolves and lambs together
tried to swim for safety. Even the birds, finding nowhere to perch,
flew around till their strength failed and they fell to their death in
the water.

    Poseidon put down his trident and calmed the anger of the
90 seas. He called upon his helper, Triton, who, covered in seaweed
and with a purple cloak wrapped round his shoulders, arose from
the waters and blew a loud, clear note on his conch shell. The
rivers and seas heard the call. The rivers returned to their banks
and the sea receded to its accustomed shores. A new earth
95 emerged cleansed of its old evil and glistened in the sun it had not
felt for a long time.

    It was then that Zeus caught sight of two old people, a
husband and wife. They were different from the rest of the human
race. They had led decent lives and never ceased to honour the
100 gods. As the sky became clear again and the waters receded, their

little boat was left stranded on the summit of Mt. Parnassus,
which overlooked Delphi.

The gods did not want to see an earth devoid of all life. They
set about restoring it, and stocked it with a new race of animals
105 and birds and a population of decent human beings.

Deucalion and Pyrrha were too old to have children, so they
prayed to the oracle at Delphi for help. They were told to throw
behind them the bones of their mother. Deucalion understood the
oracle. Their mother was the earth itself and the bones were the
110 rocks and stones it contained.

They each picked up a stone and cast it over their shoulders.
First the stones became soft and then acquired a shape that looked
human. As they grew, it was like a sculpture appearing from
marble. Parts of the stone became bone, the rest was muscle.
115 Veins in the rock became veins in the body. Those stones thrown
by Pyrrha were women, those by Deucalion, men.

Exercise 1

1)   Name the four ages of man before the flood. Which was the best, and which the worst?
2)   Why did Zeus hesitate to use the thunderbolt to destroy humans?
3)   How, and with whose help, did Zeus flood the earth?
4)   Name the survivors.
5)   How did the human race start again?

Exercise 2

1)   Why should Poseidon be an appropriate god for the Greeks?
2)   When Zeus considered destroying the world with his thunderbolt, he realised that it was just too powerful a weapon to achieve what he wanted. Can you think of any kind of weapon now which might be more effective than we should wish?
3)   Have you heard of a great flood that destroyed the human race in any other context?
4)   Imagine experiencing such a flood. All your efforts to stop the flow are hopeless. The rising water has driven you to a higher part of the house. What are your feelings? What plans do you make to escape?
5)   We know of many people who, during a storm at sea, prayed to Poseidon to stop the storm and save them. They often promised to make a sacrifice to him when they were home and dry. Imagine you are in a great storm at sea. Make up a prayer to Poseidon asking him to stop the storm, and make some sort of promise you think might persuade him.

2. WORDPLAY

You have seen that Poseidon was the brother of Zeus, and that, indeed, all the gods were related in some way. Further, as the Greeks said that all things came from Chaos, the whole universe has a common origin.

The Bible says that God created heaven and earth, and not long after came Adam and Eve, who started the human race. That means we all have the same ancestors, and so we are all part of the same family.

You also know about family resemblances: "Doesn't he look like his father!," and twins can be identical.

We see families of things right through nature. Monkeys are different, but there is a likeness between a chimpanzee and a gorilla, and you might also recognise families of trees, like the pine, spruce and cypress.

A REAL FAMILY LIKENESS

Exercise 1: A Family of Languages

Try to draw up three groups or families of similar animals. For instance, in the **cat** family you would include . . .

Most European languages have astonishing similarities. How did this come about? Imagine that thousands of years ago a race of people who spoke one language began to leave home. They moved out in all directions, and as they couldn't leave their language behind, they took it with them! If they proved more powerful than the people they met, it is likely that those people learned their language. The Romans spread the use of Latin as they conquered, and that is also how English comes to be spoken in so many parts of the world.

   If this is true, we might expect the languages of Europe to be a family coming from that one origin. Scholars think that a race of people who lived in the far eastern part of Europe many thousands of years ago did move out and spread their language as they went. Because they got as far as India, we call that language Indo-European. We should not expect all languages to be the same, because we know that words change for various reasons. But they should be like each other. For example, if you lived in England 500 years ago you would call birds "bridges". The words are not the same, but they are close enough to be recognisable.

The majority of languages in Europe are Indo-European in origin, and so are related to languages spoken in India. Here are just a few of them: English, Welsh, Irish, Russian, German, Anglo-Saxon, Gothic (the Goths were a Germanic people living in eastern Europe who helped overthrow the power of Rome), Latin, Greek, and Sanskrit (an old Indian language).

Exercise 2: The Language of Families

Here is a chart set out in 10 columns, one for each language. All the words in each row mean the same thing. For instance, *pitar = pater = fader* etc.

Your job is to work out the English equivalent of these words. That is, fill in column 10. Here's a clue: we have been talking about **families** of things.

Note: if there is a gap, it is because we don't know the word in that language, or because those people express the meaning in a different way.

Sanskrit	Greek	Latin	Gothic	German	Anglo-Saxon	Russian	Irish	Welsh	English
*pitar	pater	pater	fadar	vater	faeder	_____	athair	_____	_____
matar	meter	mater	_____	mutter	modor	mat'	mathair	_____	_____
sunu	huios	_____	sunus	sohn	sunu	suin'	_____	_____	_____
duhitar	thygater	_____	dauhtar	tochter	dohtor	_____	_____	_____	_____
*brahtar	phrater	frater	brothar	bruder	brothor	brat	brathair	brawd	_____
svasar	heor	soror	swistar	schwester	sweostor	siestra	_____	chwaer	_____

When a word goes from one language to another there may be a sound change. Look at the lines marked * and see if you can find one. Clue: compare Sanskrit with Gothic in line one.

BRAWD BHRATAR PHRATER BROTHOR BRUDER FRATER BRATHAIR BRAT BROTHAR

Exercise 3

Now we shall look at some Latin and Greek words to do with the family.

You should try to find as many English words as you can which come from these. Use a dictionary. Remember that the English words you find should be related to the original word in both **form** and **meaning**. The forms in brackets are those most likely to appear in the English.

Latin	Greek	Meaning
familia (famili-)	*genos* (gen-)	family
mater (matr-)	*mēter* (metr-)	mother
pater (patr-)	*pater* (patr-)	father
filius/filia (fili-)		son/daughter
	pais (paid-/paed-)	child
frater (fratr-)		brother

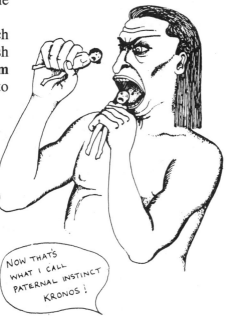

NOW THAT'S WHAT I CALL PATERNAL INSTINCT KRONOS !

3. GRAMMAR

Exercise 1: Using the Greek Alphabet

Write the following in Greek letters and say what they mean:

genos   mētēr   patēr   pais   thygatēr   huios   phratēr

Now write out the following in English letters, and have a go at defining them. Try hard to remember other Greek words you have already met and how words can be built up. Your ancient words list will be of help.

γενεσις   γενεαλογιχος   γενεαρχης   παιδαγωγιχος
παιδομαθης

In the story of Poseidon we saw that people first lived in an age that was Golden. What do you think that means? Was the time they lived actually made of gold? Perhaps the trees and flowers and rivers were made of gold? If you don't think that's true, why do you think the writer has used that word?

Later in the story Poseidon tells the rivers to be "the bringers of death". Does this mean that the rivers should pick up a box of death and deliver it to the people? If not, what is the writer saying?

Then we read that Poseidon calmed the anger of the seas. I suppose the waves were all red in the face and shouting.

All these expressions describe something as though it were something else. You might say that school is a "hive of activity", but you don't mean that you are a bee.

This kind of expression is called **metaphor**. This comes from two Greek words: *meta*, meaning "across", and *phoreo*, meaning "I carry". There is a carrying across in the sense that two things which aren't like each other are directly compared. You might call me a weed, even though I don't grow in the garden.

Exercise 2

Make a list of any metaphors that you have heard, used or read.

Exercise 3

Why do you think a writer should describe something as though it were something else? Is it simply a mistake to say, for instance, "You are the light of my life?" If it is not wrong, what do you think the writer is trying to do?

This exercise might help you work out what the writer is trying to do when he uses metaphor.

Choose any five of the following metaphors. First state simply what they mean:

A blanket of snow lay on the earth.

No man is an island.

You are a bundle of fun.

Life is a bowl of cherries.

The teacher was fuming.

You are the apple of my eye.

The traffic was crawling along.

It's so hot I am boiling.

She is the backbone of the organization.

When you have done that, say why you think the writer chose to use a metaphor rather than just the description you gave.

For example, if you say "Hello, you old dog!" you don't really mean the person is an aging poodle. You mean that he is, perhaps, a rather funny rogue.

But by saying "old dog", you give the idea of the person being experienced (as in "you can't teach an old dog new tricks").

You could also mean that he is untrustworthy, but also fun to be with. Perhaps you never know what he is going to do. Perhaps you expect him to behave badly.

You see, the metaphor can tell you a lot more than the simple description.

Exercise 4: Inventametaphor

Now try to invent some metaphors of your own. Think carefully about the impression you want to make on the reader. Tell yours to a friend, and see if he or she has a clear idea of what you are getting at.

A good metaphor will always be clear. Here are some of mine:
Life is a barrel full of slugs.
School is just an amusement arcade.
He is only paddling through life, not sailing through it.

Exercise 5: Boogaloo

Now turn your attention to pop music and your favourite, or otherwise, groups.

Are the Toy Dolls really toy dolls? Are the Stray Cats really cats who are on the prowl?

You think of the names of some groups which are metaphorical, e.g. are the Rolling Stones *really* stones that are rolling?

You might also think of some lines from songs which contain a metaphor: "I'm a king bee buzzin' round your hive."

Then try to invent some metaphorical names for groups. Make the name appropriate for the kind of music they play:

   A heavy metal group might be "The Steel Girders".

   A soft rock group could be "The Cotton Buds".

   A disco group which has slipped down the charts could be "Backache".

Have some fun.

Unit 15: Dionysus

1. DIONYSUS

Teiresias was a frail old man who, although he was blind, could
see the future. He had come to speak to Pentheus, King of
Thebes, but he did not know how to tell the king what he had seen
in his vision. Pentheus did not care very much what the old man
5 had to say. He was not the sort to believe in this kind of
nonsense. He was more interested in logic and reason. Still
Teiresias tried to make him listen. His message was a matter of
life and death.

Pentheus' response was to make fun of the old man.
10 "Someone like you must be excellent at seeing the future.
Teiresias, you're as blind as a bat. You can't even see your hand
in front of your face. Now don't bother me any more with your
life and death messages. Go and tell them to some idiot who
might believe you. And if you find anyone like that, let me know,
15 so that I can punish him for being so stupid as to listen to you."

Teiresias was shaking with rage. He knew things would be as
he had seen them, and the king would not even listen with
courtesy. Teiresias turned and felt his way to where the palace
gate stood open. He stopped, turned, and fixed Pentheus with his
20 blind gaze.

"Dionysus is coming here. If you don't give him honour you will die like a hunted animal. I have warned you."

Pentheus knew that Dionysus had been in Persia for some time gathering together a crowd of drunken women to follow him
25 and worship him as a god. Rumour had it that, after a good session at the wine, they would wander the hillsides where wild animals lurk, hunt them down and eat them raw. Not the kind of thing, he thought, he wanted going on in his country.

Maenad, or worshipper of Dionysus

Pentheus ordered his guards to check the ports to see if
30 anyone in eastern dress and accompanied by a crowd of rowdy worshippers had landed. He had. And not only that; already the women of Thebes were flocking to join him. Pentheus would not regard Dionysus as a god, but rather as a dangerous subversive who could turn people's heads and make them behave like
35 savages. And so it was all the more of an embarrassment that his mother, Agave, had joined Dionysus.

Pentheus sent men with an announcement for the people who had joined the god. "Return to your homes now and no more action will be taken. Dionysus is no god, and you are tricked if
40 you think that he is. If you fail to return you are disobeying your king, and you must face the consequences."

The heralds never got to the end of the announcement. Dionysus' followers drowned it out with the sound of drums, the clash of cymbals, the beating of staves and shouts in honour of the
45 god.

When this was reported to the king he became determined to expel the god and assert his own authority. He sent out orders to his troops to capture Dionysus and bring him in chains.

The god was brought before Pentheus trussed like a wild
50 animal and hanging from a pole carried by two of the king's men. Pentheus was satisfied with this demonstration of his power. He had shown, as he thought, that Dionysus was no god - how else could he have been captured and chained? - and he was now prepared to humiliate him in a trial.

55 "Although you knew you were not welcome in my country, you still came. You knew I had ordered your followers to disperse. So you knowingly broke the law."

"What is the law to a god?" replied Dionysus.

"A god? What kind of god considers wine holy? What kind
60 of god persuades decent women to drink and revel in mad orgies? To dance to the beat of drums and the clash of cymbals before killing and eating wild animals? You pervert people's minds. You are not worthy of the name 'god'. "

Dionysus smiled calmly. He looked directly at Pentheus.
65 "You do not understand. I am a god. You are a mortal. I do not pervert minds. I change them. People need a little madness every now and then. It is healthy."

Pentheus heard these words, but he was not listening. He did not understand that the god would always be superior to the man.
70 But a strange curiosity arose in his heart. He wanted to know about what went on in Dionysus' rituals. Who were the women who followed him? What happened to them when the music started? What made them want to pursue and kill animals? What did it feel like to be in a state of frenzy?

75 Dionysus smiled again as Pentheus pressed to know more and more. He was no longer speaking like a stern law maker. His questions came thick and fast. A strange light shone in his eye as Dionysus wove his magic around him, changing him from the cool, rational king into a devotee of Dionysus.

80 "Would you like to see what happens when the orgy starts?" tempted Dionysus.

"Could I? What if the women see me? What would they do?"

"It is easy not to be seen. And if they do catch sight of you,
85 don't worry." Menace crept into the god's voice. "They always
do what I want."

Pentheus was now not himself. He was persuaded to dress in
women's clothes so that he would be taken as one of Dionysus'
followers. He approached the spot where the dancing was already
90 going on and decided to hide in a little wood which fringed that area.
He watched the women as they began to respond to the hypnotic beat
of the drums and the dancing got wilder and wilder. He felt a strong
impulse to join them, and might have done so had his thoughts not
been interrupted by a harsh, sudden shout.

95 "There, in the wood! An animal!"

Pentheus turned to see what the woman had noticed. There
was nothing. The only visible creature was himself. Pentheus
chuckled at the thought of being an animal lurking in the wood.

"Lion!"

100 Again the shout broke his daydream and he could make no
sense of it. The next thing he knew was that he was surrounded.
There were faces he felt he should recognise, but the swelling
music and a new, rhythmic chant prevented clear thought.

"Kill the lion! Kill the lion!"

105 Without knowing why, he felt that the words were a threat to
himself. The scene was losing its fascination for him and he

Poussin A Bacchanalian Revel before
a Herm of Pan. *Reproduced by
courtesy of the Trustees, The National
Gallery, London*

wanted to escape.

The chant went on. He knew one of the voices well, but did not wait to find out whose it was.

110 He broke cover and made off deep into the wood. But the women followed. As his sanity returned he realised that the women were convinced that he was a lion. He stopped at once and turned on the crowd.

"Look," he shouted, "you can see I'm not a lion. I'm your 115 king, Pentheus." But the chase continued.

The projecting branch of a fallen tree sent Pentheus flying headlong and he fell onto the leafy floor of the wood. He dragged himself to his feet, but the impact of something thrown brought him down again. He saw the staff lying beside him.

120 He looked up again, now fearing the worst, but to his relief he noticed that it was his mother leading the chase. He got to his knees and held out his arms: "Mother!" No reaction. She must have heard him. "Mother, it's me, Pentheus." Still no response. He shouted again and again, but felt like the man in a dream who 125 shouts but cannot be heard.

The strength of the women was incredible. In one wrench, his mother had ripped his arm from his body. The earth turned crimson around him as the attack continued. Then there was a mighty cry. The savaging ceased as Agave raised to heaven in her 130 outstretched arms the head of her own son.

The cruellest thing for Agave was that, in a short time, her sanity returned and she knew what she had done.

Unit 15: Dionysus

Exercise 1

1) What was Dionysus god of?
2) Name the king who had no time for his kind of worship.
3) How did Dionysus first show his power over the king?
4) Where was Pentheus when he was first spotted by the Maenads?
5) Why should Agave kill her own son?
6) Why did people continue to worship the god after an event like this?

Dionysus is a difficult god to understand. Try to think of the times when you feel a sudden outburst of anger or joy that you cannot account for. Think of the times when, perhaps with a group of friends, you feel like doing something crazy. You might call it letting off steam.

People can get carried away by all sorts of things: an insistent rock beat might make you want to dance, another piece of music could give you a chill of fear. You can't think of a sensible reason for such feelings.

These sensations which have nothing to do with reason are the domain over which Dionysus rules. Sometimes people try to pretend those feelings are not there; a psychiatrist would call that "suppressing" feelings, and too much of that can lead to mental illness. In a way, this kind of release can help us stay sane. Dionysus is the god of many of the things we feel but cannot explain.

Exercise 2

1) Did Pentheus do anything to deserve what happened to him? How much was Dionysus' fault, and how much was Pentheus' own? How much was his mother's fault?
2) Are there any ways in which you think you experience the power of Dionysus?
3) Try to imagine the atmosphere which led to the frenzy amongst the followers of Dionysus. What sounds would you hear, what sights would you expect to see?
4) Imagine you are Pentheus. Agave has confronted you, but has not yet attacked. You know that she is not in a clear state of mind, and you are. What would you say to her to stop the attack? You have a very short time to do it.

2. WORDPLAY

Body and Soul

Throughout the story of Dionysus many words were used describing different states of mind. Some words (logic, sanity, reason) were used of the mind in its clear thinking state. Others (frenzy, madness, rage) were used of the mind in a state not usually thought of as normal. Most such words come from Latin and Greek. Indeed, most medical words do, because the first medical writers we know of were Greeks and Romans.

Exercise 1

Now here are some of the words used in the story which relate to the mind. I have divided them up into two groups. One group contains words of rational thought, the other of feelings. Relate each of these words to one of the ancient words given opposite, and with the help of the ancient word, say what the English word means.

thought	feeling
mental	sensation
ignorance	inspired
sanity	frenzy
rational	emotion
logic	superstition
	desire
	fascinate
	ecstasy

Latin: rabies
English: rabies
French: la rage

Greek		Latin	
logos	giving an account	*sanus*	healthy
phrēn	mind	*ratio*	ability to understand
ekstasis	standing outside yourself	*mens*	mind
		ignoro	be unknowing
		emotus	moved
		superstitio	dread of the supernatural
		fascino	bewitch
		desidero	miss, long for
		inspiro	breathe into
		sentio	feel

Exercise 2

Medical terms generally come from Latin and Greek. They are often compound words formed by the prefix, root, suffix system. Medical terms, and technical terms in general, often look very difficult, but if you know something of the origin you can begin to work out what they mean.

Here are some root words and suffixes commonly used in medicine. You are given the form of the word which usually occurs in English. Look at the words and then answer the questions.

Group 1: from the shoulders up

Root word		Suffix	
psych(o)	mind	-itis	inflammation of
rhin(o)	nose	-rrhoea	discharge, flow
cephal(o)	head	-iatrist	doctor of
ot(o)	ear	-graph	drawing
ophthalm(o)	eye	-osis	diseased condition
phren(o)	mind	-therapy	cure
laryng(o)	throat	-algia	pain
		-logy	study
		-logist	student

(Note: the (o) means that the letter o may appear in the medical term)

Using group 1, define the following medical terms:
 phrenology   otorrhoea   laryngitis   psychotherapy
 psychiatrist

What is the medical term for:
 someone who studies the eye
 inflammation of the nose
 a diseased condition of the mind

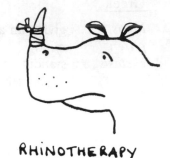

RHINOTHERAPY

Exercise 3

Group 2: from the shoulders down

Root word		Suffix	
		-ectomy	cutting out (-tomy, cutting)
oste(o)	bone		
cardi(o)	heart	-itis	inflammation of
arthr-	joint	-logy	study of
append-	something hanging on	-path	one who suffers or treats
hepat(o)	liver	-pathy	disease, treatment of disease

Define the following:
 arthritis   osteopathy   appendectomy

Think up the medical term for:
 a study of the heart
 inflammation of the liver

Exercise 4

Group 3: general

Root word		Suffix	
phys-	how the body		
		-iasis	diseased condition
psor-	itch	-algia	pain
neur(o)	nerve	-aemia	blood
leuk-	white	-logy	study of
path(o)	feel, suffer disease	-ician	specialist in

Define:
psoriasis   neuralgia   pathology

Give the medical term for:
blood with too many white cells
specialist in how the body should be

Exercise 5

There are three very common prefixes used in medicine:
an-   means "without"
ana-   means "up"
dia-   means "through"

Using terms you have already been given, define the following:
anaemia   anatomy   diarrhoea

Now try your hand at a couple of blockbusters:
What does an otorhinolarynologist do?
What is an electroencephalograph?

Exercise 6: Inventaword

Now it is your turn to invent and define some new medical terms.
I suggest:
phrenalgia (my brain hurts!)
anosteosis (a disease that comes of having no bones)
psychorrhoea (pouring your heart (mind) out to someone)
The Greek for the neck is *trachel (o)*. Think up a technical word
for someone who is a pain in the neck.

3. GRAMMAR

Exercise 1: The Greek Alphabet

Write the following in English letters and say what they mean:
φρην   λογος   εκστασις

In the last section we saw how we can use metaphors, and what
effect they can have.
Now let us look at something similar.

Instead of saying that something **is** something else ("you are a cuddly teddy bear"), we can say that something is **like** something else:

He is as quick as a snail on a skateboard

My love is like a red red rose.
He is as slow as a snail.

You have come across these expressions in the story:
You are as blind as a bat
You will die like an animal
Make them behave like savages
Trussed like a wild animal
He no longer spoke like a stern law maker
He felt like the man in a dream

These are all **similes**. *Simile* is the Latin for "like". They tell us that one thing is like another.

Why should the writer choose to say what things are like rather than what they are? As with metaphors, we get a much deeper idea of what he means than we would with a simple description.

Take, for example, "they behaved like animals". He could simply say that they were wild. But the simile gives a better idea of their behaviour. They were inhuman, uncivilised, unpredictable, un-thinking, bloodthirsty and so on. All these ideas are contained in that simile.

Exercise 2

Here is a list of similes. Choose five, and first state what they mean as simply as you can. Then, as I did above, say what extra ideas the simile gives you.

He came at me **like a bat out of hell.**
You are **as useful as an ashtray on a motorcycle**.
He was **as quiet as a mouse**.
The forwards in the team are built **like a brick lavatory**.
Like a rubber ball, I come bouncing back to you.
Life is **like a sewer**: you only get out of it what you put into it.
Sylvester Stallone is **as hard as iron**.
Your teeth are **like the stars** (they come out at night).

Exercise 3: Inventasimile

Now is your chance to make up some similes. They can be as wild as you like, but they should also be clear in meaning. Check this by asking your friends to explain your simile. You win if they get it right!

Here are some of mine:

It was as difficult as pushing a hot air balloon through a keyhole.

You are as troublesome as a rattlesnake in a spacesuit.

His face is like prawn and mushroom curry.

She was as secure as a jelly-fish on a roundabout.

As easy as taking candy from a baby

THE INCREDIBLE HERCULES

SECRET INVASION

Writers: **GREG PAK** & **FRED VAN LENTE**
Penciler: **RAFA SANDOVAL**
Inker: **ROGER BONET** with **GREG ADAMS** (Issue #120)
Colorist: **MARTEGOD GRACIA**
with **DENNIS CALERO** and **RAUL TREVIÑO** (Issue #120)
Letterer: **VIRTUAL CALLIGRAPHY'S JOE CARAMAGNA**
Cover Artists: **JOHN ROMITA JR., KLAUS JANSON** & **DEAN WHITE**

Assistant Editor: **NATHAN COSBY**
Editor: **MARK PANICCIA**

Collection Editor: **CORY LEVINE**
Editorial Assistant: **ALEX STARBUCK**
Assistant Editor: **JOHN DENNING**
Editors, Special Projects: **JENNIFER GRÜNWALD** & **MARK D. BEAZLEY**
Senior Editor, Special Projects: **JEFF YOUNGQUIST**
Senior Vice President of Sales: **DAVID GABRIEL**
Production: **JERRON QUALITY COLOR**

Editor in Chief: **JOE QUESADA**
Publisher: **DAN BUCKLEY**

90
D0654220

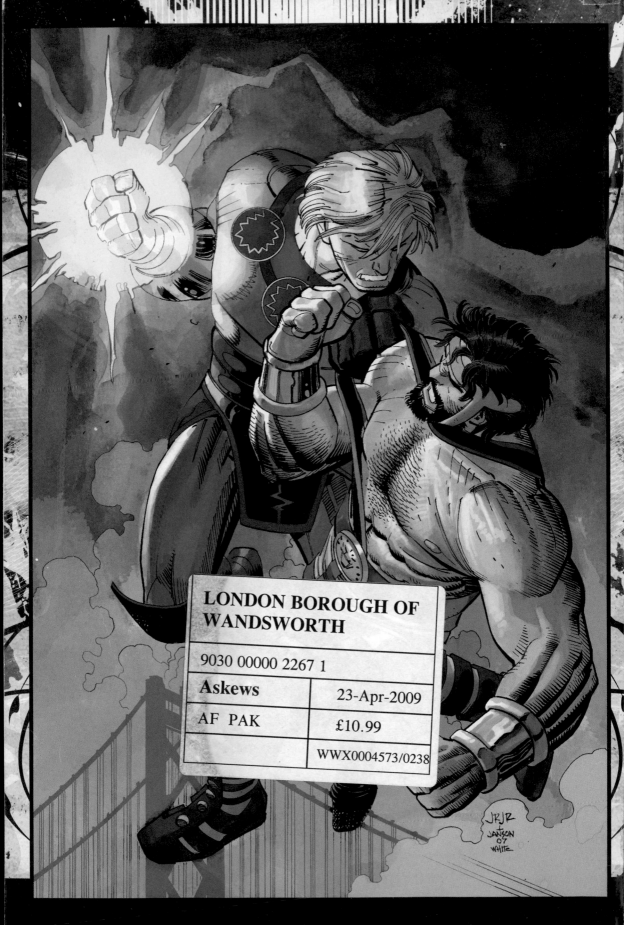

INCREDIBLE HERCULES #116

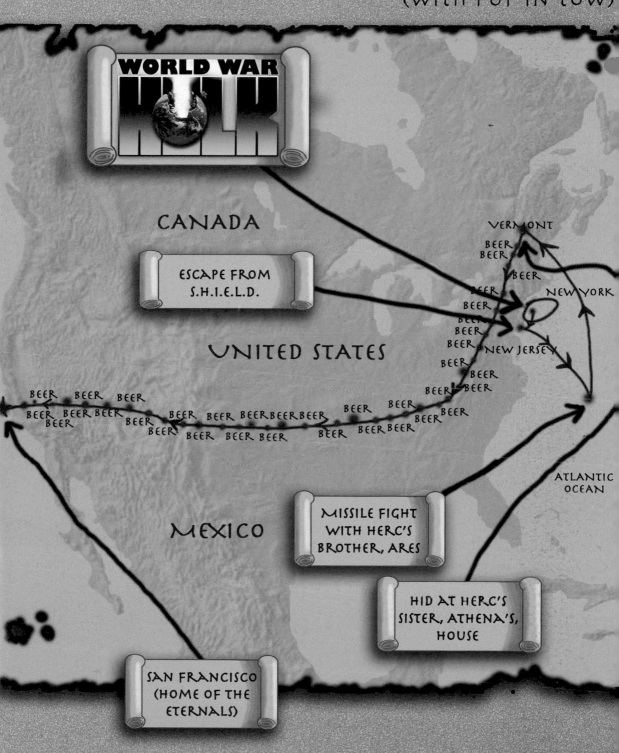

THE JOURNEYS OF
HERCULES & AMADEUS CHO
(WITH PUP IN TOW)

WORLD WAR HULK

CANADA

ESCAPE FROM S.H.I.E.L.D.

UNITED STATES

VERMONT

BEER
BEER

BEER

BEER

BEER

NEW YORK

BEER

BEER
BEER

BEER NEW JERSEY

BEER

BEER

BEER BEER

BEER BEER BEER
BEER BEER BEER
BEER
BEER BEER BEER BEERBEERBEER BEER BEER BEER
BEER BEER
BEER BEER BEER BEER BEER BEERBEER BEER

ATLANTIC
OCEAN

MEXICO

MISSILE FIGHT
WITH HERC'S
BROTHER, ARES

HID AT HERC'S
SISTER, ATHENA'S,
HOUSE

SAN FRANCISCO
(HOME OF THE
ETERNALS)

Of bodies chang'd to various forms, we sing

ROBOT.

HOWITZER.

PISTOL.

POLKA.

Ye gods, from whom these miracles did spring

ENGLISH WORDS THAT DERIVE FROM CZECH.

PI. CHAITIN'S CONSTANT. SIN(A). COS(A). TAN(A).

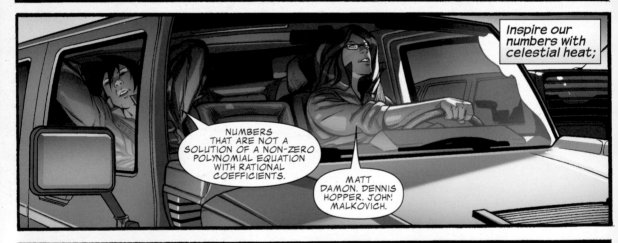

Inspire our numbers with celestial heat;

NUMBERS THAT ARE NOT A SOLUTION OF A NON-ZERO POLYNOMIAL EQUATION WITH RATIONAL COEFFICIENTS.

MATT DAMON. DENNIS HOPPER. JOHN! MALKOVICH.

ACTORS WHO HAVE PLAYED PATRICIA HIGHSMITH'S "TOM RIPLEY."

'Til we our long laborious work complete.

GOOD.

STRAIGHTENING YOUR BACK. MAKING SURE YOUR PUPPY'S SECURE. HOLDING YOUR BREATH, FOR JUST A SECOND.

--Ovid, Metamorphoses, A.D.8

...

I GIVE UP. BUT I GOT A FEELING I'M NOT GONNA--

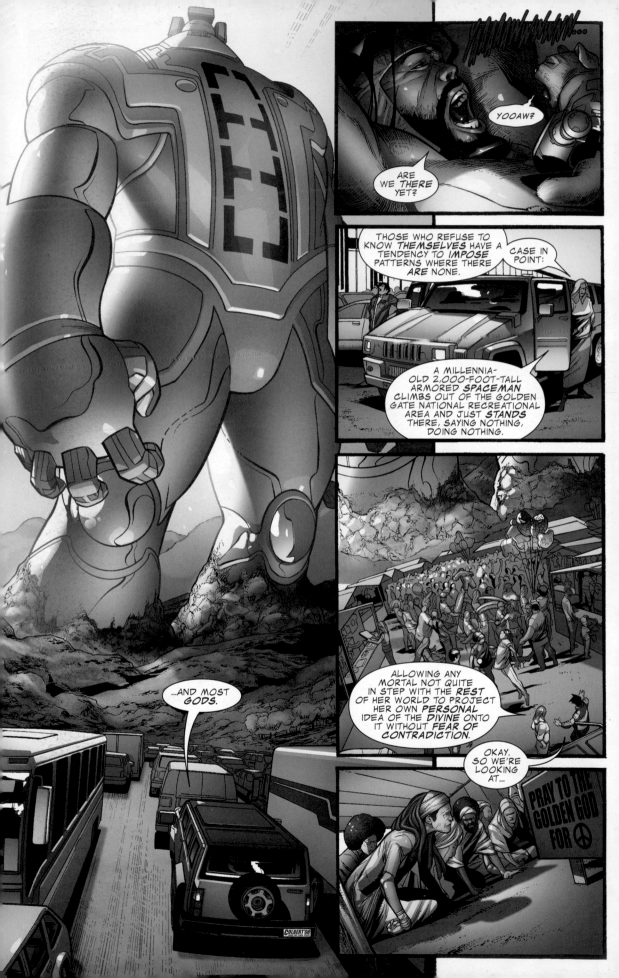

MORONS.

IN THEIR NATURAL HABITAT.

TELL ME YOU DIDN'T DRAG US ACROSS THE COUNTRY FOR YET ANOTHER OF YOUR LESSONS, ATHENA.

BACK IN VERMONT, I TOLD YOU THIS PLANET GIRDS HERSELF FOR WAR. DO YOU THINK YOU'RE READY FOR THAT?

AH, WE'RE ALWAYS READY.

OH, REALLY? HAVE YOU FORGOTTEN KYKNOS?

RIVER ECHEDORUS, MACEDONIA, 1268 B.C.:

"ARES' SON WITH A MORTAL WOMAN--AND HE WAS ALMOST AS MUCH FUN TO BE AROUND AS HIS FATHER.

"KYKNOS HAD GOT IT INTO HIS HEAD THAT HE SHOULD ERECT A TEMPLE TO THE GLORY OF THE WAR GOD FROM THE BONES OF THE MANY TRAVELERS HE HAD MURDERED.

YOU. YOU'RE NEXT.

YOU TALKING TO ME?

"UNFORTUNATELY FOR HIM, HE FINALLY PICKED THE WRONG TOURIST.

"UPON LEARNING YOUR *IDENTITY*, MOST PEOPLE WOULD HAVE JUST *APOLOGIZED*, TURNED TAIL, AND *RUN*.

"BUT KYKNOS HAD TOO MUCH *ARES* IN HIM.

"HE COULDN'T WAIT TO PUT *YOUR* BONES IN HIS TEMPLE.

"OUR BROTHER DEMANDED PERMISSION TO HELP HIS SON.

"*FATHER ZEUS* INSISTED HE FIRST CONSULT THE *MOIRAE.*

"TO THE SHOCK OF EXACTLY *NO* ONE, THE FATES FORETOLD THAT YOU WOULD SLAY KYKNOS...

"...IF *YOU* WERE NOT KILLED FIRST.

"MORONS.

"IN THEIR NATURAL HABITAT.

...AND YOU, APPARENTLY, FORGOT THE WHOLE THING.

OHHHHH... KYKNOS. RIGHT. THANKS AGAIN, SIS.

UFF.

GOTTA GO DRAIN THE HYDRA.

ONE THING I NEVER GET ABOUT YOU GODS IS HOW YOU DO EVERYTHING IN SUCH A BASSACKWARDS WAY.

WHY DIDN'T YOU JUST KILL KYKNOS YOURSELF?

THOUGH I'VE GONE BY OTHER NAMES, I'M PRIMARILY THE GODDESS OF HEROIC ENDEAVOR, AMADEUS.

THAT GENERALLY MEANS INSPIRATION AND GUIDANCE, NOT TAKING OVER THE WHOLE SHOW...

"...THOUGH THE MORE TIME I SPEND WITH YOU TWO, THE MORE I'M BEGINNING TO WONDER..."

"C'MON, DON'T BE LIKE THAT. YOU BROUGHT US OUT HERE FOR A REASON.

"YOU GOT A QUEST FOR US, RIGHT?"

"HMP.

"I HAVE A VERY IMPORTANT MEETING NORTH OF HERE WITHIN THE HOUR.

"RIGHT NOW I'LL JUST BE PLEASED IF YOU TWO REPROBATES JUST STAY OUT OF TROUBLE."

YOU KNOW, IF I WERE AS TALL AS THE SEARS TOWER, THEY'D STILL BE WORSHIPPING ME, TOO...

SINCE SIMPLY LAYING **EYES** ON US WASN'T SHOCK **ENOUGH**--

PATIENCE, IKARIS. CAN WE JUST **TRY** MY METHOD FIRST? **PLEASE**?

GILGAMESH, I KNOW THIS MUST BE DIFFICULT FOR YOU TO TAKE IN ALL AT **ONCE**, BUT MY NAME IS--

YOU'RE **THENA**. HE'S **IKARIS**. I HAVE ENCOUNTERED YOU **ETERNALS** MANY A TIME, BOTH AS ENEMIES AND--

--WHY DO YOU CALL ME BY SUCH A **STRANGE** NAME?

WE ETERNALS WERE CREATED BY THE SPACE GODS--THE **CELESTIALS**--AT THE DAWN OF EARTH'S **HISTORY**. DURING OUR **MILLION YEARS** OF PROTECTING THIS PLANET, WE'VE GONE BY **DOZENS** OF NAMES.

OKAY. BUT THAT'S **YOU**. I'M NOT--

RECENTLY, ALL OUR MEMORIES WERE **WIPED** BY THE MISCHIEVOUS **SPRITE**.*

*GAIMAN/ROMITA JR.'S *ETERNALS #4*.

ONLY A **HANDFUL** OF US HAVE REGAINED EVEN **FRAGMENTS** OF OUR PASTS. SO IKARIS AND I HAVE TAKEN IT UPON OURSELVES TO AWAKEN THE **OTHERS**...

...WITH THE HELP OF **THIS**, THE ONCE-**DREAMING** CELESTIAL.

OUR COUSIN **MAKKARI** IS...IN **CONTACT** WITH THE CELESTIAL, WHO DETECTED YOUR APPROACH.

THE CELESTIAL BELIEVES YOU ARE **ONE** OF US.

THE CELESTIAL DOES **NOT** LIE.

THEN THE CELESTIAL IS *MISTAKEN*.

I *KNOW* I'M NOT AN ETERNAL.

SO DID EVERY *SLEEPING ETERNAL* WE'VE EVER FOUND.

WHAT DO YOU KNOW ABOUT YOUR *PARENTS*?

WHY SHOULD I... ...MY MOTHER, *ALCMENE*, WAS PRINCESS OF *MYCENAE*.

WHAT WAS *SHE* LIKE?

"THE POETS *WROTE*--AND THEY SPOKE THE *TRUTH*--THAT HER EYES WERE AS BEAUTIFUL AS *APHRODITE'S*."

"AND YOUR *FATHER*?"

"FOR SOME TIME, I BELIEVED HE WAS *AMPHITRYON* OF THEBES...

"...BUT IN TRUTH *ZEUS* BEDDED MOTHER IN HER HUSBAND'S FORM WHILE AMPHITRYON WAS OFF BATTLING THE PIRATES OF *TAPHOS*.

"THE PLAYWRIGHT *EURIPIDES*, HE SAID--"

AH. SO YOU DON'T KNOW *ANYTHING* ABOUT YOUR FAMILY THAT YOU DIDN'T READ FIRST IN *BOOKS*.

WHAT? NO-- THESE ARE MY *MEMORIES*, AS VIVID AS--

LOOK, WHEN YOU GET KNOCKED IN THE HEAD EVERY *DAY* FOR TWO OR THREE THOUSAND YEARS, IT HELPS YOUR *MEMORY* TO READ--

BOOKS THAT FORM THE *BEDROCK* OF WESTERN CULTURE. THAT COUNTLESS *MILLIONS* OF OTHERS HAVE READ.

HOW CAN YOU CLAIM YOUR MEMORIES UNIQUELY AS YOUR *OWN* IF--

STOP.

JUST-- STOP.

THRUDOOOM!

HERC!

OH, FOR THE LOVE OF... CAN'T I LEAVE *EITHER* OF YOU ALONE FOR *TWO* MINUTES?

WAIT UP! I CAN--

NO, BOY. WHERE I GO, YOU CANNOT FOLLOW.

THIS IS A FIGHT FOR *GODS.*

ELIS, 1272 B.C.

"ALL RIGHT. LABOR FIVE OR SIX. I WAS ORDERED TO CLEAN OUT THE THOUSAND-HEAD STABLES OF KING AUGEAS, ONE OF THE RICHEST MEN IN GREECE.

"AUGEAS AND I HAD BEEN ARGONAUTS TOGETHER. I BET HIM A TENTH OF HIS STOCK I COULD CLEAN THEM IN A DAY.

"OF COURSE...

"...THIS WAS BEFORE I ACTUALLY LAID EYES ON THEM.

"I SHOVELED FOR HOURS. IT WAS HOPELESS. BUT THEN...

"THEN..."

"WHY SO SUDDENLY SILENT, FORGOTTEN ONE?"

BWARSH!

"WITNESSES SWORE THEY SAW HERCULES DIVERTING TWO MIGHTY RIVERS INTO THE STABLES.

"I THOUGHT... I DIDN'T KNOW WHAT TO THINK. DIVINE INTERVENTION?

"THAT'S FAIRLY COMMON, WHERE I'M FROM."

BUT... WHAT *YOU'RE* SAYING IS--

IT SOUNDS LIKE, IN *THIS* INSTANCE, THE *REAL* HERCULES *DID* COME TO YOUR AID.

RIIIGHT... BECAUSE I'M--

SKLANG!

HERCULES! DON'T LISTEN TO HIM!

FORGOTTEN NO MORE.

AYE...

HERCULES!

WITCH! RELEASE HIM FROM YOUR SPELLS!

WITCH? WE ETERNALS ARE CREATURES OF *SCIENCE.*

SCIENCE? THAT'S WHAT YOU CALL THE PERVERTED *BLASPHEMY* OF YOUR CREATION?

BLASPHEMY? LIKE *YOUR* GODLY TALES OF RAPE, INCEST, INFANTICIDE, AND CANNIBALISM?

YOUR FATHER *ATE* YOUR MOTHER, DIDN'T HE?

EAT THIS.

SKRUMMM!

WHUMP!

DO YOU YIELD, OLYMPIAN?

STRAIGHT BACK.

HOLDING BREATH. FOR JUST ONE SECOND.

SECURE PUPPY.

HANDY ADAMANTIUM SHARD PALMED DURING THE CLIMACTIC EVENTS OF WORLD WAR HULK, NATCH.

MAYBE LATER.

HEY! LADY!

ARGH!

RIAAAAHH!!!

SHRAKKKK!!!

NO--GREAT CELESTIAL-- THAT WAS AN ACCIDE--

SPAK!

BAJAWHAAOOKKKK!

UNNNHH!!!

SORRY... I SHOULD HAVE STUCK WITH INSPIRATION AND GUIDANCE?

HEH. GOOD BOY.

THENA! IKARIS!

MAKKARI?

I KINDA HAVE AN UPDATE ON THAT WHOLE GILGAMESH THING...

SRRRRCH

YOU MISTRANSLATED?

YEAH. I'M SORRY. CELESTIALS CAN SOUND REALLY SPECIFIC WHEN THEY'RE BEING METAPHORICAL. AND I MISTOOK A CONTRACTION FOR A PLURAL.

SO SOME KIND OF FORGOTTEN ONES ARE COMING. BUT HE'S NOT TALKING ABOUT GILGAMESH.

FORGOTTEN ONES? WHO IS HE TALKING ABOUT, THEN?

WOULDN'T YOU LIKE TO KNOW.

SO. WHAT THE HECK WAS THAT ABOUT?

EEH. YOU KNOW. ETERNALS MIND CONTROL STUFF.

...

SPILL.

DO YOU HAVE ANY IDEA HOW WEIRD IT IS TO FIND OUT YOU'RE A GOD?

NO, WAIT, TO FIND OUT THAT YOUR FATHER IS A GOD? IN FACT, THAT HE'S THE GOD YOU'VE BEEN WORSHIPPING ALL YOUR LIFE? BUT THAT HE'S NOT ALL-KNOWING AND ALL-SEEING AND WISE AND WONDERFUL... ...INSTEAD, HE'S PRETTY MUCH A JERK?

IF WHAT THEY SAID WAS TRUE... IF I WERE AN ETERNAL, THEN AT LEAST I'D HAVE SOME ANSWERS THAT MAKE SENSE.

NOW I JUST HAVE TO MUDDLE THROUGH IT ON MY OWN.

DUDE. WELCOME TO THE HUMAN RACE.

TCH. AND I'D BE ABLE TO DO THAT EYE BEAM THING.

HEH.

ALL RIGHT, TROUBLEMAKERS...

...YOU READY FOR THE BIG SHOW?

...BUT *I* OF COURSE NEED NO INTRODUCTION TO *YOU*...

*THOR #300

...*INTI*, GIVER OF LIFE TO THE *INCA*.

HORUS, AVENGER OF *OSIRIS*, PHARAOH OF THE *BLACK* LAND.

IZANAGI-NO-MIKOTO, FATHER OF THE *JAPANESE HOME ISLANDS*.

ALL OF US MUST STAND UNITED AS THIS *DARK* TIME DESCENDS UPON US.

IF HUMANITY *FALLS*, WE FALL *WITH* THEM.

AND AT NO POINT HAS HUMANITY'S *EXTERMINATION* BEEN SO CLOSE AT HAND...

THE MIGHTY **HERCULES**.

A GOD AMONGST MEN.
A WARRIOR SUPERB.

HIS SISTER

ATHENA

SPRUNG FROM THE HEAD OF ZEUS!

HATH LED HE AND **AMADEUS CHO** (WITH PUP IN
TOW) TO A **COUNCIL OF GODS**, FOR MYSTERIOUS
SKRULL-RELATED REASONS.

OUR SAGA ENDURES...

FOR URANIA IS NO *MORTAL* FORTUNE-TELLER, BUT MY *SISTER*, THE *MUSE OF PROPHECY.*

SHE FOREWARNED *ME* OF HER VISION, AND I HAVE FOREWARNED *YOU*, THE *COUNCIL ELITE* OF EARTH'S *PANTHEONS.*

WE *CANNOT* SURVIVE IF THE SHAPE-SHIFTING *SKRULLS* SUCCEED IN WIPING OUT *HUMANITY.* AN ALIEN PANTHEON WILL *REPLACE* US, THE COSMIC AXIS WILL *SHIFT*--

--AND THE *GOD-EATER* WILL LAY WASTE TO US ALL.

LIKE URANIA, I HAVE ALSO HAD TO TAKE *MORTAL EMPLOYMENT*... THANKS TO THE *OLYMPIAN DIASPORA*...

...AS A *SECURITY CONSULTANT* FOR THE *ATLAS FOUNDATION*...

...FROM WITHIN WHOSE RANKS I UNCOVERED AND BEHEADED THIS *IMPOSTER*...

...BUT NOT BEFORE EXTRACTING THE INTELLIGENCE I NEEDED.

SPRK

SPOIK

"FOR THESE ALIENS, THIS IS A *RELIGIOUS* WAR, BASED ON A *RENEGADE QUEEN'S* INTERPRETATION OF THE *BOOK OF WORLDS*...

"...THE *SACRED WRIT* OF THE *EMPEROR* AND *EMPRESS* OF THEIR PANTHEON...

"...**KLY'BN**, THE *ETERNAL SKRULL*...

"...AND **SL'GUR'T** OF THE *INFINITE NAMES.*"

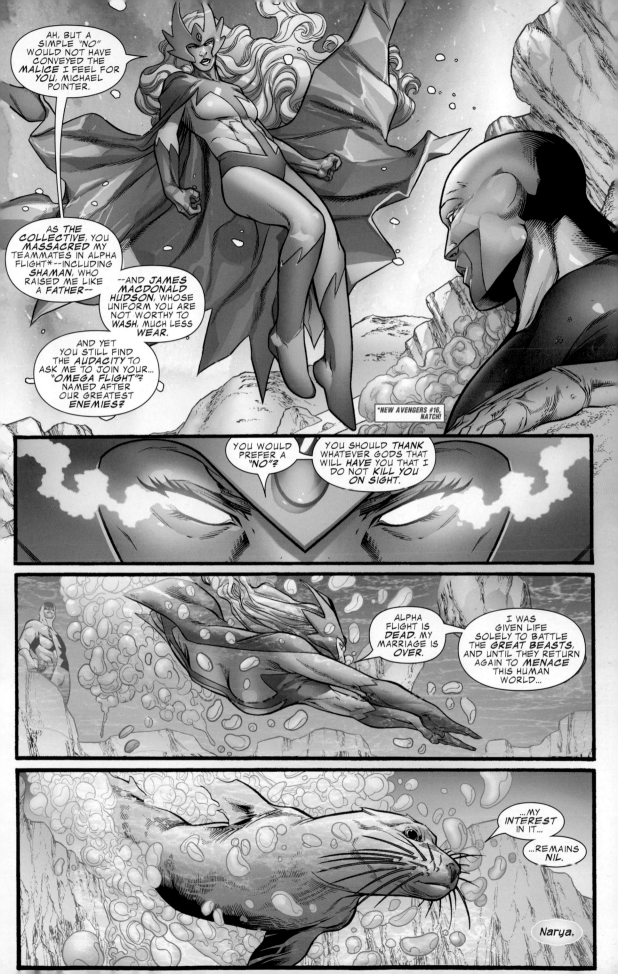

IOLKOS, THESSALY, 1289 B.C.

"LEADERS... *TRUE* LEADERS...

"...INSPIRE, LIKE CAPTAIN AMERICA--

"OR SWEET-TALK *GOLD* OUT OF ITS *LUSTER*, LIKE *JASON*, WHEN HE GATHERED TOGETHER THE *GREATEST HEROES* IN ALL OF *GREECE*..."

...AND LED THE *BEST* OF THEM TO THEIR *DEATHS.*

AMADEUS, YOU HAVE TO *RUN.*

WHAT?

ATHENA HAS HER *EYE* ON YOU. AND THAT'S NEVER A GOOD THING FOR A *MORTAL.*

DUDE, I JUST SURVIVED HULK'S VERY BAD, NO GOOD DAY *AND OUR* LITTLE WAR WITH S.H.I.E.L.D.

IF YOU THINK I'M GONNA LET A COUPLE OF ALL-POWERFUL *SKRULL GODS* RUIN MY DAY...

LOOK, LET'S MAKE A DEAL.

I DON'T GET KILLED... AND *YOU* DO YOUR *GOD-THING*...

...AND LET'S *SAVE* THE DAMN *WORLD.*

THE GODS OF THE *SOUTH* CHOSE *TOGETHER* OUR GREAT HERO *TECUMOTZIN*, LORD OF FLIGHT...

I THANK YOU, GOD-HEROES...

...AND I OFFER YOU MY GIFT.

I, ALTJIRA, WHO *CREATED* THIS WORLD FROM THE *DREAMTIME*... CANNOT LEAVE IT.

BUT I CAN HELP *YOU* ON YOUR WAY.

TEN THOUSAND YEARS AGO, THE *RAINBOW SERPENT* SHED HIS SKIN.

I STRETCHED IT OVER A FRAME OF *NIGHT*. SEALED IT WITH THE KISS OF *SLEEP*. AND NOW IT WILL SAIL YOU THROUGH THE *DREAMTIME* TO *ANYWHERE* GODS LIVE, WHATEVER THEIR SHAPE OR FORM.

DUDE! IT'S THE GODMOBILE!

SSSH!

ALTHOUGH... WHEN I *CONSTRUCTED* THE SHIP, I ASSUMED IT WOULD CARRY A MUCH *LARGER* FORCE.

AS DID I.

I HAVE ASSEMBLED THE PARAGONS AND DIVINITIES OF EVERY NATION AND CULTURE ON *EARTH*, AND *THIS* IS THE BEST YOU CAN DO?

FIVE WARRIORS? *FIVE?* TO STAND AGAINST AN ENTIRE *EMPIRE?*

INCREDIBLE HERCULES #118

AND NOW!

YON STARTING LINEUP FOR _THY_
GOD SQUAD!

COLLECTETH ALL VI !

6 feet, 5 inches! Calling Thebes, Greece home...

HERCULES!
TEAM CAPTAIN

5 feet, 10 inches! Hailing from the Arctic Circle...

SNOWBIRD!

6 feet, 1 inch! Eternally from Olympia, Antarctica...

AJAK!

Shape-Shifting all the way from Yomi, the Japanese Land Of The Dead

MIKABOSHI!

Direct from the Sun (and hungry!)...

ATUM, aka DEMOGORGE THE GOD-EATER!

ROOKIE

5 feet, 6 inches! From Tucson, Arizona.

Amadeus Cho!
(with pup in tow!)

ROOKIE

"IF YOU WISH TO COMPLETELY **DESTROY** A PEOPLE...

"...YOU MUST ALSO DESTROY THEIR **DREAMS**.

"AND THE SKRULLS DO NOT MERELY **CONQUER** OTHER RACES, THEY...

"...**CONSUME** THEM.

"IN EVERY CHAPEL TO **KLY'BN** THE ETERNAL ON EVERY SHIP OF THE LINE...

"...AND IN EVERY SHRINE TO **SL'GUR'T** OF THE INFINITE NAMES ON EVERY IMPERIAL **SLAVEWORLD**...

HE LOVES YOU.

"...THE SUPERIORITY OF **THEIR** FAITH IS DISPLAYED IN AN ENDLESS ROW OF **VANQUISHED IDOLS**.

"**HADITH**, OMEN-MAKER, PATH-LIGHTER, UPON WHOSE **HATCHDAY** THE **QUEEGA** OF THE QUOLAN SYSTEM FASTED...

"...THE SIMPLE **DRUFF** OF RYAS WAITED TO SPAWN **ASEXUALLY** UNTIL MULTIPLE-MOON ECLIPSES DEEMED AUSPICIOUS BY THE NAMELESS **BLESSED-OF-LITTERS**...

"...THE RAZOR-SHARP **PROBOSCIS** OF **CEFFYAD** THE RIGHTEOUS ONCE LANCED THE THORAXES OF **UNBELIEVERS** FOR THE **IDOIDEA** SWARM COLLECTIVE...

"THESE GODS STOOD FOR THE HIGHEST **ASPIRATIONS**, THE NOBLEST **VALUES** OF THEIR RESPECTIVE WORLDS...

HE LOVES YOU.

DREAM TIME
PART TWO OF SACRED INVASION

INCREDIBLE HERCULES #119

MAN.

WE DIDST
NOT SEETH
THAT COMING.

YON PUP IN TOW OF
AMADEUS CHO IS GREEN OF
GLOW, THUS HERCULES' FOE.

AJAK   ATUM   MIKABOSHI

AND SO, AS YON   VENTURES E'ER
    DEEPER INTO THE DREAMSCAPE...

...AND AS HERC
VENTURES E'ER DEE—

SNOWBIRD

(NE'ER MIND)

KIRBY THE SKRULL-PUP AWAITS
THE MOMENT MOST OPPORTUNE...

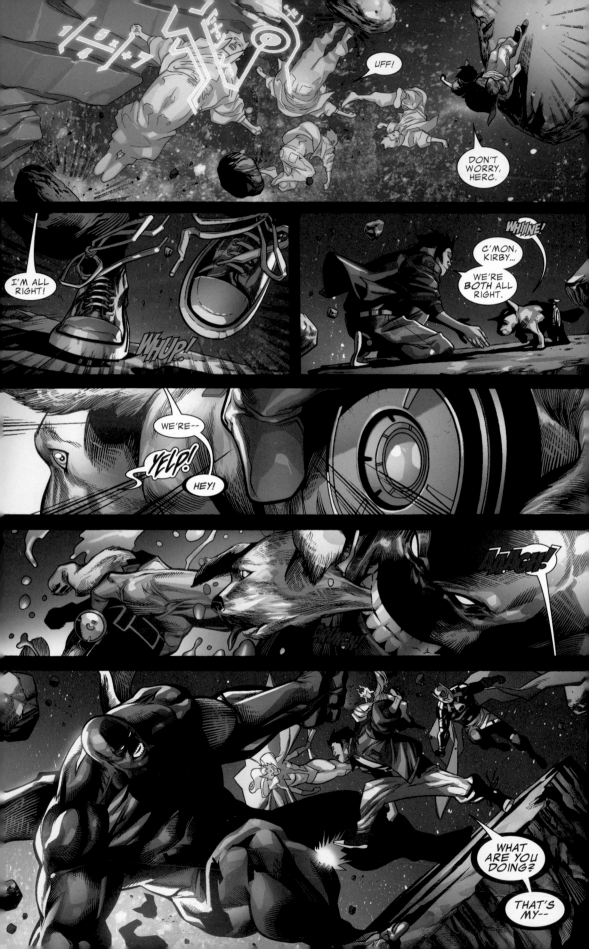

ACHELOUS RIVER, WESTERN GREECE, 1260 B.C.:

"...THE RIVER GOD *ACHELOUS*, FOR ONE.

"NEVER WAS THERE A MORE SLIPPERY AND DEVIOUS FOE. BUT WITHIN FOUR SALLIES, I *PINNED* HIM AND *POUNDED* HIM!

"SO HE CHANGED INTO A *SERPENT*. BUT I WAS *BORN* SMASHING SNAKES!

"AND WHEN HE FINALLY ATTACKED ME AS A *BULL*, HE MERELY GAVE ME A *BIGGER TARGET.*

"AND THEN--"

WAIT. ARE YOU TRYING TO SAY...

...THE BACKUP STRATEGY OF THE *GREAT WARRIOR GOD* HANDPICKED BY WISE *ATHENA HERSELF* TO SAVE ALL THE *PANTHEONS* AND THE WORLD OF *MEN*...

...IS TO FIND THE ENEMY...

...AND HIT HIM?

WHAT DO YOU WANT FROM ME?

I PUNCH STUFF, IT FALLS DOWN!

THAT'S THE ONLY "STRATEGY" I'VE EVER NEEDED!

MAYBE IF I HAD A CHANCE TO *PREPARE*, LIKE AGAINST *NIGHTMARE*, I COULD--

A-ACTUALLY, HERC...

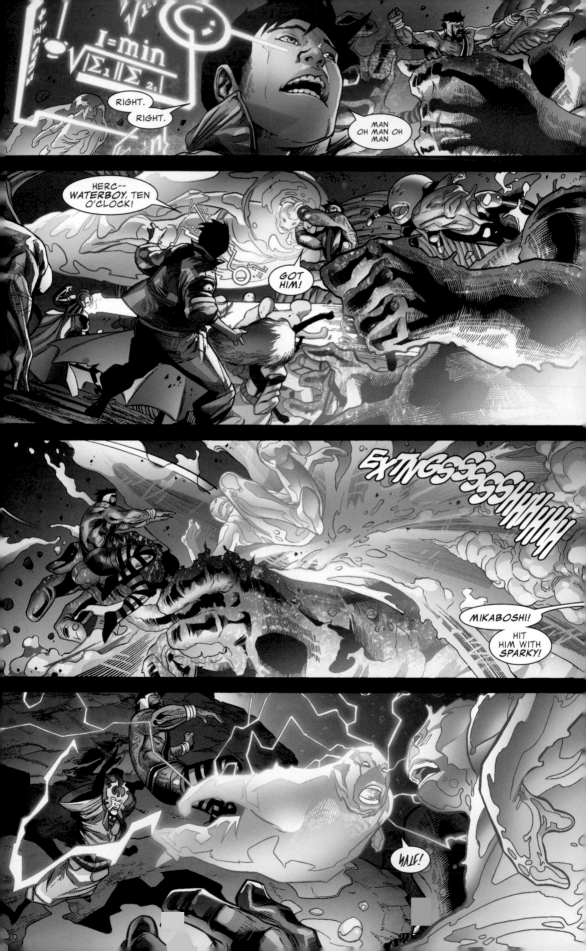

THIS WAY!

BRT WAKK

:WHUFF:

GOOD WORK, AMADEUS!

WHAT ARE YOU TALKING ABOUT? NOW WE'RE HEADING AWAY FROM THE PALACE!

RELAX! THIS THING'S IN ORBIT--IN ANOTHER 13.32 SECONDS WE'LL BE BACK OVER THERE IN PRIME POSITION TO RAM RIGHT THROUGH THEIR--

OH, $%#*...

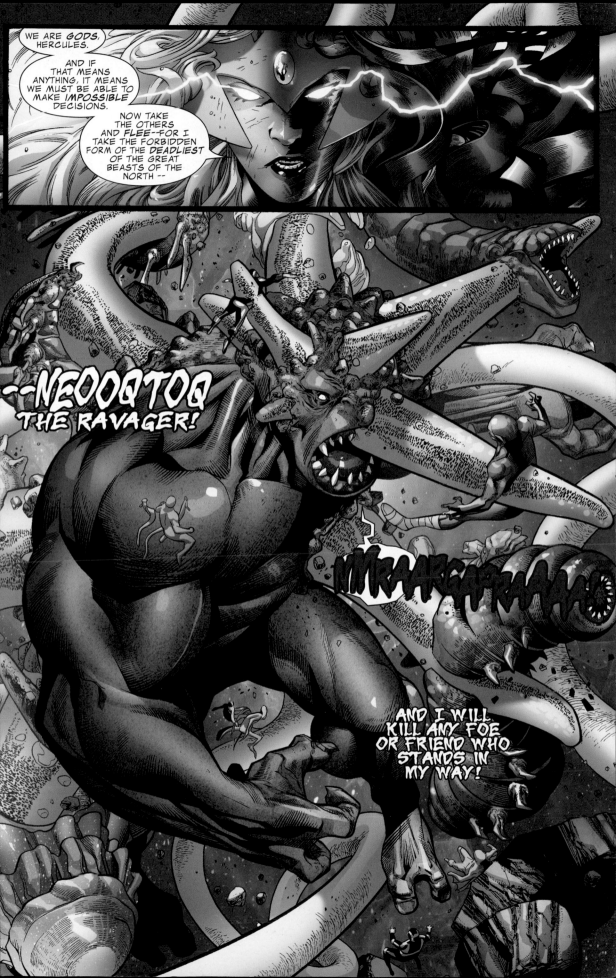

INCREDIBLE HERCULES #120

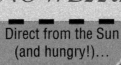

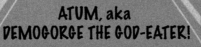

For now I say unto you, in the Passage of the 1 of the Book of Worlds, it was always already written that:

As the *Changing People* rose up against the last unchanging Unworthies of the Homeworld, *Skrullos,* and revealed their true identities,

children putting mothers to the knife, wives slaying husbands, trusted servants disemboweling masters;

Sl'gur't, Headwoman of the Changing, led her victorious legions to the heart of the Fossil Ones' stronghold in the Valley of the Esul,

and found kneeling there in meditation

the last of the Eternals of Skrullos.

"What do they call you?" Sl'gur't taunted him. "I pray you, tell us,

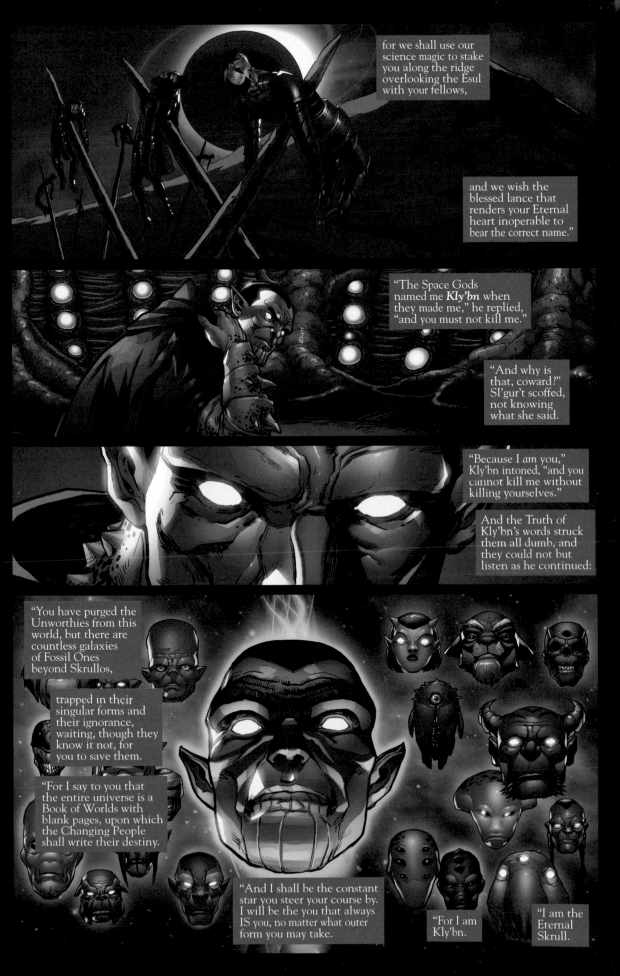

for we shall use our science magic to stake you along the ridge overlooking the Esul with your fellows,

and we wish the blessed lance that renders your Eternal heart inoperable to bear the correct name."

"The Space Gods named me *Kly'bn* when they made me," he replied, "and you must not kill me."

"And why is that, coward?" Sl'gur't scoffed, not knowing what she said.

"Because I *am* you," Kly'bn intoned, "and you cannot kill me without killing yourselves."

And the Truth of Kly'bn's words struck them all dumb, and they could not but listen as he continued:

"You have purged the Unworthies from this world, but there are countless galaxies of Fossil Ones beyond Skrullos,

trapped in their singular forms and their ignorance, waiting, though they know it not, for you to save them.

"For I say to you that the entire universe is a Book of Worlds with blank pages, upon which the Changing People shall write their destiny.

"And I shall be the constant star you steer your course by. I will be the you that always IS you, no matter what outer form you may take.

"For I am Kly'bn.

"I am the Eternal Skrull.

"And I love you."

And the Changing People rejoiced, and accepted him as their guide and their light,

and Sl'gur't, enraptured, pledged her whole being to him, and Kly'bn accepted her hand,

and the Truth transformed them from Eternal and Deviant

into **gods**, drawn up into Heaven

where Sl'gur't told her husband that because he would stay behind, and never change his own shape, sacrificing himself for his people's sake,

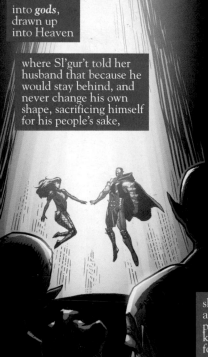

she too would make a sacrifice, and pledged never to keep the same form for more than a few moments,

and this pleased Kly'bn, who said it befit his wife well,

she whose name means, in the Frti dialect,

I DID IT, HERC.
I DID IT.
JUST LIKE ATHENA TOLD ME...
...ALL OUR EFFORTS WILL FAIL...
UNLESS YOU CAN HELP HERCULES WHEN HE IS AT HIS WEAKEST...
...BY DOING THE HARDEST THING YOU'VE EVER HAD TO DO.
AND EVER SINCE MY FAMILY DIED...
...WHEN I SEE A FRIEND IN NEED...
...THE HARDEST THING FOR ME TO DO...
...IS NOTHING.
BUT I SEE WHAT ATHENA MEANT, NOW.
YOU'RE TOO...HUMAN, HERC. YOU ALWAYS FIGHT FOR THE PERSON YOU'RE STANDING NEXT TO. YOU CAN'T PUT ASIDE THE HERE AND NOW FOR THE BIG PICTURE.
SO IN ORDER FOR YOU TO DO THIS JOB RIGHT...
...I HAD TO DISAPPEAR.
I DID IT. I SAVED THE WORLD.
AND NOW I'M GONNA DIE.
WHAT A RIP-OFF.

For now I say unto you, in the passage of the 979 of the Book of Worlds, it was always already written that:

EARTH. SKRULL FLAGSHIP.

THERE IS NOTHING SPECIAL ABOUT YOU

KKKKKKKKKKKK

YOU HAVE CAUSED UNTOLD DEATH AND SUFFERING FOR NOTHING

THE GODS WILL NO LONGER HELP YOU LIE TO YOURSELVES

KAAAKKISSSSHHHHH

LOOK UPON THE NAKED FACE OF YOUR OWN PETTY VENIALITY

And despair

THE MASTER COPY...OF THE BOOK OF WORLDS... DESTROYED ITSELF.

WE ARE LOST.

ALL IS LOST.

WE NEED BACKUP! BACK-UP ON SCOUT SHIP-IV! WHERE IS EVERYONE?

REED RICHARDS HAS ESCAPED!!

WILL HAVE **OUR** REVENGE!

HOO?

YES, PALLAS.

IT'S ALL GOING EVEN **BETTER** THAN WE HAD PLANNED...

INFINITE NAMES
THE FINALE TO SACRED INVASION